LANG'S
COMPENDIUM OF
CULINARY NONSENSE
AND TRIVIA

LANG'S COMPENDIUM OF CULINARY NONSENSE AND TRIVIA

BY GEORGE LANG

An
amusing,
helpful,
vital,
trivial,
surprising,
shocking,
revealing,
I-knew-it-all
collection of
facts,
fancies,
and fantasies.

DESIGNED AND ILLUSTRATED BY MILTON GLASER

Clarkson N. Potter, Inc./Publishers New York
Distributed by Crown Publishers, Inc.

Copyright © 1980 by George Lang
Illustrations copyright © 1980 by Milton Glaser
Introduction copyright © 1980 by William Safire

Inquiries should be addressed to Clarkson N. Potter, Inc.,
One Park Avenue, New York, New York 10016

Printed in the United States of America

Published simultaneously in Canada by General Publishing Company
Limited

Library of Congress Cataloging in Publication Data
Lang, George, 1924–
   Lang's Compendium of culinary nonsense and trivia.
   Includes index.
   1. Food—Anecdotes, facetiae, satire, etc.
I. Title.   II. Title: Compendium of culinary
nonsense.
TX353.L33   1980   641   80-16284
ISBN: 0-517-541483

10 9 8 7 6 5 4 3 2 1
First Edition

Previously published selections by George Lang have appeared in different form in: *Bon Appetit*,
Copyright 1976, Bon Appetit Publishing Corp., *Esquire*, *International Review of Food & Wine*,
Restaurant Hospitality, and *Travel & Leisure* magazines.

*Gratitude (and all sorts of credit) should go
to my associate of a decade, Adele Rodgers,
to whom this little book is dedicated.*

George Lang

CONTENTS

*Culinary history is a collection of questionable
happenings, recorded by persons of dubious
credibility, about events no one cares about
and people of no consequence.*
    —anonymous twentieth-century compendium writer

I NTRODUCTION
by William Safire

Words about people involved with food begin with "g."

A *gourmet* is a connoisseur of extraordinarily discriminating taste; a *gourmand* is a hearty eater who delights in good food and drink and occasionally stuffs himself; a *gastronome* is an expert in the art or science of dining and wining; a *glutton* is a slob who never knows when enough is enough.

George Lang is a gourmet and a gastronome; I'm a gourmand; we're both gluttons for punishment. He traipses around the world, designing hotels, creating national cuisines, running world's fair pavilions, launching restaurants, running for Renaissance Man; I churn out words about words. We were brought together by Grace Kelly, then newly married and freshly princessed, who never met either of us: George was then assistant banquet manager of the Waldorf-Astoria, and I was program chairman of the Overseas Press Club. Somebody asked us at the club if we wanted to host a luncheon for Prince Rainier and Princess Grace; I said sure, we like to give royal parties, and called the Waldorf.

"I want to give a luncheon for about three hundred people this Friday, and we can't afford more than six dollars a head," I told the guy who announced himself as "Lang."

He had a good laugh at that. "The Waldorf is booked solid

three months in advance. And your budget is out of the Dark Ages."

"Okay," said I. "We'll give this lunch for the Prince and Princess of Monaco someplace else. You know another hotel?"

Then Lang went into action. Perhaps for the prestige, perhaps because his boss, Claude Philippe, was an admirer of the former Miss Kelly, perhaps because George liked a challenge—whatever the motive, the Lang approach was something to see. A nice bunch of ladies who had booked the Starlight Roof years before were told the room had suddenly become unworthy of them; they were broken into smaller groups and sprinkled around the hotel. The hotel chef outdid himself, turning out a meal fit for a princess and three hundred of her closest friends; a menu especially appropriate to Monaco was designed; the chandeliers were washed; napkins and tablecloths reflected the nation-state's colors; strolling violinists did their thing—and all for six bucks a throw. The Fourth Estate never had it so good.

Since then, George Lang has made a name for himself in the world of food and hostelry, awakening the American Dream—from a standing start as a refugee from Hungary in the forties to the top of the heap in the eighties. He now entertains his friends by playing his own Stradivarius in the most dramatic apartment in Manhattan. Why? Because he made a habit of creative enthusiasm.

14

Example: I invited a flock of friends, including George, to an outdoor cookout. Making proud, hostlike noises, I put the steaks on the grill; then it started to rain, hard. I gathered up the wet slabs of meat and took them back inside to the kitchen to stick in the broiler. The meal was going to be a disaster—no charcoal flavor, no pizazz, just ordinary meat probably overcooked and boringly presented.

"All right, give me a few tomatoes," George Lang said, in his Grace-Kelly-Is-Coming-and-We-Can't-Afford-to-Act-Like-a-Pack-of-Nerds voice. He slammed the meat around in the broiler, muttering something about getting it all in the middle to take advantage of convection currents. He grabbed some spices out of the cabinets and did a thing with them on the meat. Then he took a dozen tomatoes and built a pyramid in the middle of a tray; when the steaks were ready, he laid them along the sides of the pyramid, making the main course look like a crown, a genuine *pièce de résistance* (a French term for a solid joint of meat, its substance offering resistance to the fork and resistance to quick consumption, as all gourmand lexicographers know). All the guests gasped at the imagination of the presentation; the rain-washed meat was not as tasty as it might have been, but that was not George's fault.

15

Read this book the way you would work over a table of smorgasbord. An anecdote here, a recipe there, a morsel of history on the side. Rinse it down with a good book about wine.

LANG'S
COMPENDIUM OF
CULINARY NONSENSE
AND TRIVIA

OYSTERS
FOR
BREAKFAST

CHAPTER

1

T-Birds

NE FRIED COFFEE TO GO

I enjoy eating breakfast. I enjoy the olfactory anticipation of coffee, the taste of sweet butter on crunchy thin toast, the casual glimpse of headlines in the morning rag, and the anticipation of another day full of surprises and possibilities. Perhaps Sydney Smith was right also when he said that no one is conceited before one o'clock.

Here is an arbitrary selection of morsels and snippets about this stomach-warming subject, collected throughout the years.

Oyster Breakfast

One of the greatest gourmands of all time was Grimod dé La Reynière. His grandfather died in 1754 on the battlefield—that is to say, at the dinner table, having eaten himself to death on *pâté de foie gras de Strasbourg.* (As epicures everywhere will agree, what a beautiful way to go!)

He had a tasting society that was so difficult to get into even Talleyrand didn't make it. Here is an excerpt from his *Almanach des Gourmands* (1803):

> Oysters are the usual opening to a winter breakfast—indeed they are almost indispensable. But this is often a dear introduction through the indiscretion of guests who generally pride themselves on packing them by the hundred in their vain-glorious stomachs. Insipid pleasure, which brings no real enjoyment, and

> often embarrasses an estimable host. *It is proved by experience that, beyond five or six dozen, oysters certainly cease to be enjoyable.*

A Venetian Breakfast

Begin with a *Vermouth Amaro* in lieu of a cocktail. For hors d'oeuvres have some small crabs cold, mashed up with sauce tartare and a slice or two of *prosciutto crudo*, cut as thin as cigarette paper. A steaming risotto with *scampi*, some cutlets done in the Bologna style with a thin slice of ham on top, hot Parmesan, and grated white truffles, and *Fegato alla Veneziana* complete the repast except for a slice of *stracchino* cheese. A bottle of Valpolicella is exactly suited to this kind of a repast and a glass of fine champagne and ruby-coloured Alkermes for the lady, if your wife accompanies you, make a good ending. The maître d'hôtel will be interested in you directly when he finds that you know how a man should breakfast.

from THE GOURMET'S GUIDE TO EUROPE, Lieut.-Col. Newnham-Davis and Algernon Bastard, 1903

Tom Sawyer's Breakfast

While Joe was slicing bacon for breakfast, Tom and Huck asked him to hold on a minute; they stepped to a promising nook in the river-bank and threw in their lines; almost immediately they had their reward. Joe had not had time to get impatient before they were back again with some

22

handsome bass, a couple of sun-perch, and a small catfish—provision enough for quite a family. They fried the fish with the bacon and were astonished; for no fish had ever seemed so delicious before. They did not know that the quicker a fresh-water fish is on the fire after he is caught, the better he is; and they reflected little upon what a sauce open-air sleeping, open-air exercise, bathing, and a large ingredient of hunger makes, too.

from TOM SAWYER by Mark Twain, 1876

23

A Breakfast at Delmonico's Circa 1893

The estimable Charles Ranhofer, chef of the famous Delmonico's restaurant in New York City of yesteryear, listed eight complete breakfast menus for each month of the year. Here is a random sample of dishes offered:

Caviare canapés
Sea bass with almond butter
Codfish tongues with chopped sauce
Truffled pig's feet
Guinea fowl with sauerkraut
Broiled bear steak
Turkey wings with turnip
Broiled ptarmigan
Rum omelet
Small green turtles, baked

Fried Coffee

Jim Nelson recalls his father taking him fishing on the lake owned by an old farmer. Jim wrote: "Your new cook book floats a pleasant aroma all the way down here. And speaking of that, have you ever heard of fried coffee? The old farmer charged us 50 cents a day for a boat and fishing privileges, with coffee thrown in. The last phrase is accurate. He literally threw ground coffee into a frying pan, added some water and held it over a wood fire. 'A breakfast drink,' Jim concluded, 'fit only for the demons who live deeper than hell!'"

from **FRIED COFFEE AND JELLIED BOURBON by Willan C. Roux, Barre Publishers, 1967**

Stomach-Debilitator

Coffee, as used on the Continent, serves the double purpose of an agreeable tonic and an exhilarating beverage, without the unpleasant effects of wine.

Coffee, as drunk in England, debilitates the stomach, and produces a slight nausea. In Italy it is made strong from the best Coffee, and is poured out hot and transparent.

In England it is usually made from bad Coffee, served out tepid and muddy, and drowned in a deluge of water, and sometimes deserves the title given it in "the Petition against Coffee," 1674, page 4, "a base, black, thick, nasty, bitter, stinking Puddle Water."

25

from THE COOK'S ORACLE, by William Kitchiner, M.D., 1838

Breakfast Fantasy

In my opinion a well-developed breakfast fantasy can be more interesting than many people's sexual fantasies. Here is mine: Sophia Loren would be my breakfast partner. As we listen to a lyrical little baroque *aubade* brilliantly performed by the Guarnieri quartet, Peter Ustinov would bring in warm brioche (baked by Gaston Lenôtre) and comment on the news of the day. The dean of astrologers would quietly predict delicious little surprises which await someone who was born on July 13.

No phones would disturb, of course, during the breakfast ritual, but a specially printed newspaper would be presented—full of cheering good news. One of the courses would definitely be an immensely rich Marmite full of baby vegetables, pheasant, and little quail eggs. The fruit basket would contain rambutan from Bali, mangosteen from India, perfectly ripe mangos from the Philippines, fraises des bois from southern France, and peeled giant gooseberries from my parents' garden in Hungary. Instead of coffee, we'd sip "iron goddess of mercy" tea, which grows only in a few steep mountains of Amoy in China and used to be harvested by trained monkeys.

I do think my dream breakfast is more delicious than the one Washington Irving dreamt of: "dainty slapjacks, well buttered and garnished with honey and treacle."

 ## IRD MANIA WITH DIM SUM

If you are expecting to read about English girls in a Chinese joint in London's Chinatown, stop your reading right now. This story is about real birds and real *dim sum* in the *Hing Wan Teahouse* at 119 Queens Road Central in Hong Kong. From the outside the shop looks like any other small, open-front Chinese tea shop. But if you are one of the initiated and go between the hours of 7:30 A.M. and 9:00 A.M., and walk past the tearooms on the street level and second floor, up to the third floor, you'll find yourself in a large sunny room filled with Chinese men, tea, circulating *dim sum* carts (the delicious little dumpling snacks), and a prevalence of birds in exquisitely carved little cages.

What brought these people here? And the birds?

In Hong Kong, many shopkeepers, clerks, laborers, and retired people keep birds as pets. Before going to work they combine breakfast (a cup of congee or *dim sum*) with a bit of gossip and take the birds for their daily socializing session.

For thousands of years, a Chinese gentleman's day started with the formal exercise of *Tai Chi Chuen* (always under a tree); a bit of music played on one of the traditional musical instruments; and finally an outing with his pet bird to a nearby teahouse.

At the Hing Wan Teahouse an ageless man in gray, baggy Bermuda-length shorts brings in an aluminum bowl, two tiny cups, and a cup of tea (four or five kinds are available); if you are a real aficionado, first you pour hot tea in the metal bowl and rinse your tea cup before pouring the tea into it. The tea will be very strong as is customary in the morning in China.

If you eat snacks on the ground floor, tea is free; on the second floor it's about fifteen cents, and on the third floor it's eighteen cents—to compensate for the birds, I guess.

People take a few of the little dumplings served in steamer

baskets as they pass by and between bites they feed their birds grasshoppers purchased at the entrance door. The bamboo cages are exquisitely carved and are all slightly different in color and decoration. Depending on the master-carver and the elaborateness of his design, and even such details as the graining of the wood (much as with handcrafted violins), these cages can cost from $300 to $750 each. One I saw had a little kidney-shaped feeder with an engraved sterling silver cover and cost over $3,000, probably representing the entire savings of a lifetime.

Many of the people here are of the age when thoughts have already turned from passion to pension, and their faces are etched with many scores of years' experience. The birds are their hobbies, and often the discussions visibly and audibly become very agitated (probably arguing about the good points of their birds, touting them like horse owners in Kentucky). In the meantime the birds exchange greetings—coquettish birds with impertinent tails, vain canaries flattered by attention, little yellow-bellied feathered creatures with hypnotic stares, some sounding like Joan Sutherland, others mumbling their lyrics—but all of them clearly enjoying the morning outing.

Most of the bird cages rest right on the little tables, but some hang in the windows and on rods built between the columns.

This lovely indulgence is by no means limited to the elderly and the lower classes. A friend of mine, a well-known restaurant tycoon, goes home in the afternoon (to interrupt his sixteen-hour working day) and, after taking a cool shower, he sits in front of his pet birds and listens to them rapturously.

Leaving, as I pass the bare-chested cooks in the miniature serving kitchen (not much has changed since the early Ching Era), I think I know the answer to the ancient Greeks' dilemma about whether a perfectly executed Alexandrine line is prettier than the singing of the birds . . .

29

OEDIPUS WRECKS:
FOODS in HISTORY
CHAPTER
2

RAISE APOLLO AND
PASS THE TESTICLES

When I worked with the eminent hotelier
Claude Philippe at the Waldorf-Astoria in the
1950s, I was continually awed by the elaborate
preparations for his "April in Paris" ball. Once I discussed
with Elsa Maxwell, who was co-creator of the ball with
Philippe, the fact that it was all done even more
extravagantly about 2,000 years ago at the house of the
Roman gentleman, Trimalchio. Here is the scene as
Petronius describes it:

After a bath, everyone proceeds to the dining room of the
house, singing loudly. Young Alexandrian servants pour
snow over the guests' hands (to refresh them) while the
appetizers are served. The elaborate dishes include
miniature sausages sizzling on individual silver grills with
plums and pomegranate seeds underneath, to imitate coals.

I don't care what you call it it'll never fly

Then a basket is brought in with a wooden chicken sitting in its center. Trimalchio lifts the chicken up and finds some "eggs" under it made of pastry. Inside the pastry eggs are tiny figpecker-birds, ready to eat.

Servants enter with a silver skeleton (so real it seems to be walking by itself) while 100-year old Falernian wine is poured on hands and dripped into the mouths of the guests.

A huge circular tray displaying the twelve signs of the zodiac is brought in. Next to each sign are corresponding foods: fried testicles and kidney pairs over the Heavenly Twins; sow's udder with Virgo; a bull's eye with Sagittarius, etc. Servants then remove the upper tier of the tray to reveal stuffed capons and a hare fitted with wings to look like Pegasus. Four servants pour a spicy sauce from wineskins over fish swimming around in—what seems like—the stream of the dish.

While Trimalchio delivers a learned monologue about astrology, a giant wild boar on a platter is brought in on a litter, followed by a pack of hounds. Baskets filled with dates are suspended from the boar's tusks, and dumplings made to look like piglets at suck surround the animal. A flock of thrushes fly out from underneath and are caught and distributed to the guests.

While the music is playing, tables are cleared and three raw white pigs are brought in decorated with muzzles and bells.

The cook is summoned because he dared to serve them without gutting and roasting them first. He is stripped, ready to be severely whipped, but everyone pleads for mercy from Trimalchio. During the commotion, the cook cuts open the belly of the largest pig and out come roasted sausages, blood pudding, and other appetizing charcuterie.

While waiting for the next course, there is a lottery with prizes awarded for the best improvised puns. Then the ceiling suddenly starts to rattle and the entire dining room shakes. The ceiling opens up, and gifts and money rain upon the guests.

Sex and explicit sensuality were never far from the Roman dining table. A baked pastry likeness of Priapus, the god of phallus, is brought in on top of other cakes and buns, with apples and grapes representing his testicles. Everyone grabs for them greedily, but as a practical joke, saffroned liquid spurts into the face of anyone who touches.

35

Hell of a party, Trimalchio

The floor is scattered with golden and scarlet sawdust while slaves imitate the sounds of rare birds to please the guests. Just to make sure that the scene doesn't remain *too* tranquil, other slaves break in, quarreling and smashing dishes on each others' heads. During these spectacles, guests are showered with flowers, massaged with scents, and finally Trimalchio reads his last will and testament. (For Romans death was always nearby and was faced matter-of-factly, not feared.)

Famous gastronome Grimod de La Reynière was known for his astonishing appetite and bizarre parties. At one, for instance, the guests ate with their hands in the Roman style and then wiped them on the loosened hair of half a dozen pretty maids dressed in white togas. At another memorable dinner, the food was served on a catafalque in a black-curtained room illuminated with hundreds of

candles. To remind his guests of the brevity of life (and thus the importance of living it fully), the seat of each guest was an open coffin. I hesitate to speculate on what foods were served at this dinner . . .

Parties in the royal houses of Europe could also be characterized by excess in food and display. One of the most revealing stories I can recall was told to me by someone whose grandfather was a minor official at the court of Franz Josef. On certain occasions His Royal and Imperial Majesty disliked the movement of food servers, so the Master of Ceremonies came up with a perfect solution: behind each guest stood a server, and then another server every three feet all the way to the kitchen. A human chain was ready to pass the food from the chef to the guests and back to the kitchen. This way everyone received his food or wine without any unnecessary moves.

37

SHALL I WRAP UP THE CRAYFISH, MR. APICIUS?

Athenaeus wrote extensively about the Pompeiian gentleman Apicius, who "spent myriads of drachmas on his belly." When he heard during an after-dinner conversation that a certain place in Africa had exceedingly good and very large crayfish, he reportedly "sailed thither without waiting a single day, and suffered exceedingly on his voyage." When he arrived after weeks of sailing, the fishermen came alongside in their boats and offered to Apicius some fine crayfish specimens. He asked them if they had any finer inland, and when they said no, he purchased all the crayfish and ordered the captain of the ship to return to Italy without going ashore.

38

PICKLE MAKERS AND CASSIA FLOWERS

No other culture in the world is as food-oriented as the Chinese. This was already apparent by the second century in the personnel roster of a book of rituals called *Chou li*. Out of almost 4,000 persons who had the responsibility of running the king's residential quarters, 2,271 (or almost sixty percent) handled the food and wine. Of these, 162 were master dieticians in charge of daily menus of the king, twenty-four were experts on preparing turtle and shellfish, and six occupied themselves exclusively making pickles and special sauce.

In the Ming Dynasty (1368–1644), a fleet of barges was used to deliver the delicacies of the Yangtze province and those of the south to the palace in Peking. The Directorate of Foodstuff had priority on canal facilities. A historian of the era in 1917 noted that fresh plums, the fruit of the strawberry tree, fresh bamboo shoots, and shad were kept fresh on 1,500-mile journeys by ice blocks wrapped in straw. Some of the other items sent by barge should indicate the level of royal gastronomic sophistication: cassia flowers for seasoning, swans, cherries preserved in honey, and flaky pastries filled with marrow.

Chinese poet-gourmet Yuen-mei in his book *Shih tau* (1814) wrote probably the most precise guide to the principles of cooking, and the pursuit of excellence combined with pleasure, through dining. He even went so far as to advise on the percentage of attention one should give to different aspects of a dinner. There are twenty pages alone on how to choose the proper vinegar for different dishes! Chefs of today's nouvelle cuisine would have felt quite at home there, using their wild raspberry vinegar on thinly sliced raw eel.

39

OME TO ME, WHOSE STOMACH CRIES OUT . . .

Soup has existed as long as mankind. The whole business started when Esau, in a well-publicized transaction, exchanged his birthright for a lentil potage.

It took many years and messy revolutions to get to the point today where you can find almost any variety of mass-produced soup in a can or envelope on your supermarket's shelf. To understand the road that led to this glorious state of affairs, we must actually go back in history to medieval France.

By the fifteenth century, France had developed a series of guilds, each controlling certain areas of the food business. The *rôtisseurs* could make and sell spitroasts in their own shops; the *charcutiers* were the cold pork-meat pâtés and sausage vendors; the *poulaillers* had the exclusive right to sell raw poultry, game, eggs, cheese and such; the *sauciers* provided all sauces for the meats sold by other guild members; the *pâtissiers* sold pastries and meat pies baked in pastry; the *boulangers* the breads; but the common denominator was the fact that everything they sold was taken away from their shops and eaten off the premises.

Traiteurs formed the only group allowed to cook and serve entire meals on their own premises or at social functions—like weddings—in the home of the client. The *cabaretier* came closest to today's restaurateur; he provided properly set tables and food (purchased from other guild member specialists) to accompany the wine and other spirits served to guests in attractively decorated public rooms.

After the French Revolution, many things changed besides the form of government. In 1765 on rue des Poulies, a certain Mr. Boulanger opened an eating establishment which offered his own soups, a category not controlled by the various licensed guilds. Simple marble-top tables, an ambiance which was charming but devoid of the luxury offered by *cabaretiers* and *traiteurs*, and, apparently, a pretty cashier girl made the place an instant success. The sign over Mr. Boulanger's soup shop read in Latin: *Venite ad me omnes qui stomacho laboratis et ego restaurabo* — "Come to me, whose stomach cries out and I will *restore* you." Thus the restaurant as well as its name was born as we know it today, and it all started with soups.

41

I have always had an affinity to soups of all kinds. I love to cook and eat soup at any time of the day. When, a few years ago, eleven of us were asked to contribute a chapter to a cookbook, I naturally chose the soup chapter. Once I even cooked a five-course soup dinner for a friend who loves soup as much as I do—though I must say I stretched the point when it came to dessert, serving *Zuppa Inglese*.

History is full of believe-it-or-not soup trivia. Examples?

Rice soup, which was made with dried fruits, honey, and milk in the Middle Ages, gradually became thicker and thicker. Finally in the nineteenth century it became rice pudding.

The ancient Greeks served lettuce soup at the end of a meal because it was supposed to be sleep-inducing. According to ancient Roman gossip columnists, Emperor Domitian purposely served lettuce at the beginning of state dinners, hoping to torture all guests who, of course, couldn't fall asleep in front of their Imperial Majesty.

In the Court of Louis XI, the ladies were so vain that they lived almost exclusively on broths and consommés because they thought that chewing food would distort the face by developing ugly facial muscles.

The all-American chowder is actually of French origin.
When French fishermen emigrated to New England,
they filled their *chaudière* (a large, heavy soup and stew
pot) with the riches of the Atlantic Ocean, and thus their
matelote, bourride, bouillabaisse, and *cotriade* soups
became a variety of different American chowders,
notably clam chowder.

Posthumous gossip: Louis Diat, chef of the Ritz in New
York, supposedly invented vichyssoise, remembering his
mother's delicious potato and leek soup (so many chefs
imitate their mother's cooking, with mixed results, that
perhaps we should accept the possibility that "Oedipus
wrecks"?). Mr. DeGouy, a rival chef and author, had
another explanation of how vichyssoise came to be.
According to him, this peasant soup was first served to
Louis XV. The king was so suspicious of his cooks that he
would not touch any food until a variety of official testers
had tasted it first. As a result, this cream of leek and potato
soup arrived lukewarm and the king would not eat it,
saying, probably sarcastically, that it was "not cold
enough." Someone in the entourage quickly chilled it and
thus vichyssoise was born. Or was it?

43

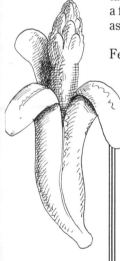

SPARAGUSMANIA NOW

Some people accuse me of having an asparagus fetish; if loving the taste, the subtle difference in shape, and the possible taste combinations of this food means this, then so be it. As a form of confession, I might as well issue a page from my asparagus trivium, to be published posthumously.

Few people know, for instance that

it belongs to the lily family.

it used to be called, according to Theodora Fitzgibbon, "sparrow grass" in England up until the eighteenth century.

Louis XIV gave a title and land to Jean La Quintinie, who invented a method of supplying asparagus to the king all year around.

you can make paper out of asparagus as well as ice cream.

there are many types of asparagus and its color ranges from snow white (Belgium) to purple (Italy).

ninety-four percent of its weight is water.

the Romans invented the idea of cooking it standing up (so that the delicate tips could be left out of the water and not overcooked), and this is still the best way of cooking it.

H ORS D'OEUVRES À LA ST. BARTHOLOMEW

Pliny, the Roman historian, called artichokes a "fashionable conceit," but it took fifteen centuries for them to become a staple of the Italian diet. Friendly vendettas were waged over which region produced the best varieties, and no other garden vegetables fetched such a high price.

A fifteenth-century Italian novel described artichokes as an aphrodisiac "dear to Venus." Perhaps this fed the sexual appetites of Catherine de Médicis, Madame Du Barry, and many of the "horizontal ladies" in search of food which gives pleasure twice.

45

Antonius Musa, physician to the Roman Emperor Augustus, wrote a lengthy treatise about the plant, specifying its effectiveness against forty-eight diseases. Although twentieth-century doctors will only admit that it's rich in iron and iodine, what do they know about these things . . .? It was supposed to be good for the digestion. Eaten before drinking, it hindered drunkenness and, taken after, it cleared the head. So, before going back to the office

one for the road

after a three-martini lunch, consume at least one artichoke! Worn around the neck it protected one from evil spirits (it was planted in churchyards for this purpose).

Historically, the Greeks started the whole thing, or perhaps the Chinese, depending on which historical gossip column you read. If you want to play twenty questions (trivia for those in the younger generation) you may use these tidbits:

> Jefferson brought the artichoke to the United States from Italy while on an expense account trip abroad.
>
> Jerusalem artichoke is a different thing altogether.
>
> the black magician who started the St. Bartholomew's Eve Massacre in 1572 ate several dozen artichokes beforehand.
>
> the word artichoke is derived from the Arabic *al-Khurshūf*, which in the Algerian slang became *carchouf*, in Spanish *alcachofa*, in Sardinia, *iscarzoffa*, in Italy *carciofo*, which in English in the Middle Ages became *archychock*, and from there we know what happened, although I have a feeling by now you know more about artichoke etymology than you care to.

Culinarywise, you should know that certain lucky areas in France and Italy have very small, tender baby artichokes which, thinly sliced, can be eaten as fresh relish.

46

There is a most unusual delicacy in Rome called *carciofi alla Giudea*. The entire artichoke is flattened with a wooden utensil and crisp-fried so you may eat the entire globe.

There are over 300 different preparations in the classic cuisine for artichokes, ranging from the simplest (and best) method of boiling the whole artichoke and dipping its leaves into clarified butter, mustard, or vinaigrette sauce, or perhaps a homemade lemon-mayonnaise, to nineteenth-century taste-scrambles like artichokes stuffed with *foie gras*, purée of wild mushrooms, and truffles.

G IUSEPPE, THEY'RE PLAYING OUR SONG

I have read about turnspits that were operated by dogs in the Middle Ages and had

Hard of hearing chef waiting for the roast to finish

one myself (bought at a street market in Aix-en-Provence) which rang a bell when the time came to remove the meat. But recently I found the mention of a musical turnspit used in the kitchens of the Count de Castel Maria of Treviso, Italy, which not only turned 130 roasts at the same time but played a number of tunes as well. When it came to certain parts of the song, the chefs knew it was time to remove the meat from the spit. I wonder if the song was, "Love Makes the World Go Round"?

48

 # ROTHER, CAN YOU SPARE A DIME FOR A POUND OF CAVIAR?

The seventeenth century didn't think much of caviar. Mouffet, whose early seventeenth-century manuscript gives us lots of information about period tastes (enough to write a melodrama), says: "As for cavialie, or their eggs, being poudred, let Turks, Grecians, Venetians and Spaniards celebrate them ever so much, yet the Italian proverb will ever be true:

Chi mangia di caviale   He who eats caviar
Mangia moschi, merdi e sale. Eats flies, shit and salt.

IQUID ASSETS

Château Carbonnieux produces one of the best dry wines in the Graves district of Bordeaux. Apparently the Turkish court liked it so much that in the seventeenth century, to get around the Koran's restriction against alcohol, with the Sultan's permission the wine was labeled *Eau Minérale de Carbonnieux*.

The water provided by cities in olden days was usually muddy and full of objects that didn't belong in any self-respecting liquid—it was rather like finding bones in chocolate pudding. One of the few exceptions was a Tea-Water Pump in New York, which provided crystal-clear drinking water "suitable for making tea" throughout most of the eighteenth century.

49

Although an obscure Muslim trader mentioned it as early as the ninth century and Marco Polo made a passing reference to it, the first time tea came to the attention of the West was in a learned three-volume book published in Venice titled *Navigatione et Viaggi* by a gentlemen named Hajji Mohammed. He called the reader's attention to a drink in China called *Chai Catai*: "Those people would gladly give a sack of rhubarb for one ounce of *Chai Catai*. And those people do say of Catai that if in all parts of the world, in Persia, and the country of the Francs, people only knew about it, there is no doubt that the merchants would cease altogether to buy rhubarb."

No wonder tea gained in popularity, especially in England. One character in Charles Dickens's *Pickwick Papers* (1836–1837) said: "There's a young 'ooman on the next form but two 'as drunk nine breakfast cups and a half; and she's a-swellin' wisibly before my wery eyes." It sounds as if she liked tea more than rhubarb.

WEET TALK

Sugar penmanship, which can be both functional and decorative in pâtisserie and confectionery, has just one advantage over conventional writing—its three-dimensional quality can be much more dramatic. Most other aspects are disadvantageous, especially the fact that soon after it's made, it disappears like yesterday's snow.

The history of pastry-calligraphy is rather recent. Unfortunately, it had neither a sixteenth-century master like Ludovico degli Arrighi to write an all-encompassing book of instructions, nor a contemporary master like Hermann Zapf to inject today's character into this specialized art form. Although Marie-Antoine Carême (1784–1833) is generally considered to be the greatest chef in culinary history—he was chef for Talleyrand, the Prince Regent (later George IV), Czar Alexander I, and Baroness Rothschild—his most notable invention was the

introduction of an architectural style into the art of pastry.
Yet neither he nor his immediate successors used
calligraphy in their extraordinary pastry exhibitions.

51

It is difficult to pinpoint the exact date when the first writing on cakes occurred, but most probably it was in 1830. This was the year that the great sugar baker, Franz Sacher, created his famous torte for Prince von Metternich and, on top of the smooth chocolate glaze, wrote his own name with delicate hand. From then on, the countries of the Danubian Valley, especially Austria and Hungary, invented cakes for celebrities and important occasions with the appropriate inscription as ornamentation.

The next step came some time in the 1920s when personalization became fashionable. In fine households even the dusting cloths were monogrammed. Although everyone obviously knew the names of the bride and groom, lovely plaques appeared as part of the wedding cake, and soon after anniversary, birthday, and holiday inscriptions became common.

Like a child discovering the limitless possibilities of a particularly good toy, chefs began to make increasingly elaborate decorations for cakes. On an anniversary cake, for instance, they might even copy the original wedding certificate. Once in an exhibit in Cologne, I was amazed to see a faithful replica of the cover of the Gutenberg Bible!

A cake calligrapher has to make his own pen and ink. For a "pen," he usually prepares a paper tube the shape of a cone, generally cut from a triangular piece of parchment. (It is also possible to use a pastry tube with a metal point, called an icing bag, which will make a different design based on the shape of the opening.) The "ink" is the so-called royal icing, made essentially with egg whites and powdered sugar whipped together with a pinch of cream of tartar. There are also various kinds of creams used and even, horribile dictu, a chocolate plastic paste.

What makes royal icing indispensable to ornamental decoration and calligraphy is that after the soft pastelike material is applied, it hardens to the consistency of plaster.

Although sugar was known in Europe from the end of the fifteenth century, it was the most expensive and rarest of foodstuffs. As a matter of fact, it was only sold in pharmacies as a medicine. As a sweetener of foods and beverages, it was only used from the beginning of the eighteenth century.

53

After Benjamin Delessert began to produce sugar commercially from beetroot at the beginning of the nineteenth century, cakes and tortes became part of the standard culinary repertoire. Royal icing dates from this time too.

Gingerbread, which is thought to have been invented by an ancient Greek baker from Rhodes, was often gilded with decorative calligraphy. The art developed differently in various countries. Perhaps the most interesting gingerbread was made in the shape of a book, with an alphabet written on it so children could learn to spell the easy way. What an ideal way to solve the "why Johnny can't read" problem!

LAUDE, PAINT ME A DOZEN NAPOLEONS!

Puff pastry, or *mille-feuille*, was probably invented by Claude Lorrain, the great seventeenth-century landscape painter, the master of light. He began his life as an apprentice to a pastry cook in Italy, where he apparently stumbled upon the technique of folding butter into pastry.

HE CASE OF THE MISSING INGREDIENT

My children's adopted grandmother, Etel Salacz, was brought up in northern Hungary where entertaining guests was a way of life. Elaborate dinner parties, afternoon teas with delicate, lighter-than-air cakes, were as much part of a girl's upbringing as learning to dance, playing the piano, or doing petit point.

An accurate recipe for a special dish or cake was sought after with the zeal of a good stock-market tip. Our Mimi (as we all call her) learned early in life the importance of being nice to people, and she wasn't surprised at all that when someone asked her mother for the recipe of an especially splendid torte her mother obliged readily.

55

For her eighteenth birthday, Mimi received a volume of the collected family recipes. But—and here's the point of our story—she was told that a single ingredient or step was missing from each one. No one who asked for these recipes could get the same result—quite obviously. All the missing pieces were recorded in a *separate* volume. Mimi was instructed not to part with certain things precious to a girl, and second on the list was the secret-ingredient booklet.

Anyone born in central Europe toward the end of the last century has lived through several wars and revolutions. Mimi lost a lot of things before leaving her homeland, but one of the things she regrets the most is the irreplaceable little book of missing ingredients.

In case you come across a red Morocco leather volume with a little silver clasp, and you see in it something like this—

Father's Favorite Chocolate Cake
3 tablespoons of bread crumbs must be added to the basic mixture

—please get in touch with us without a moment's delay.

WORD of MOUTH: A HOPELESSLY INCOMPLETE GUIDE TO THE ORIGINS of DISHES

CHAPTER 3

IMLET

The perfect proper gimlet was the invention of a British naval surgeon, Sir T. O. Gimlette, who was concerned that gin was affecting the efficiency of the naval officers, especially when the ship was in stormy weather. By mixing lime juice with the gin, he theorized, they would be able to navigate through hell and—especially—high water. No one kept records, but gin mixed with Rose's Lime Juice (half and half, please, and stir only once) remains a pretty good drink, even on modern-day dry land.

UNJAB PUNCH

Liquid puzzle: What's the connection between the Indian province of Punjab and a rum punch? Answer: this northwestern section of India is named after its five rivers (*pancha* means five in Sanskrit), and punch is named after the fact that it always contains five ingredients (alcohol, water, lemon or lime, sugar and spice). It was introduced to England toward the end of the seventeenth century by intelligence officers of the British Navy.

ARTINI

In 1871 the British Army adopted the Breechblock single-shot rifle of the Swiss inventor, Friedrich Von Martini. First called the Martini Henry, it eventually became the "Martini."

In Rudyard Kipling's *Barrack Room Ballads*, there is a ballad called "The Young British Soldier." One stanza goes:

When 'arf of your bullets fly
wide in the ditch,
don't call your Martini a
cross-eyed old bitch;
She's human as you are—you
treat her as sich,
An' she'll fight for the
Young British soldier.

The martini had great stopping power, with a correspondingly violent recoil, giving rise to the descriptive "kick of a Martini." When some brave soul added dry vermouth to his gin, perhaps as a change from gin and tonic, he found it had the "kick of a Martini," and Martini it became.

—J. K. McDowell of Garden City, N.Y.

There is no such thing as a single martini

In 1650, young Thomas Martin and his pretty wife, great with child, settled in a flourishing community in a verdant valley of central Vermont.

In the course of constructing an extra room for the happy event, Thomas fell from a crude scaffold and struck his knee on a jutting stone. By next morning, it was alarmingly swollen, and when over the next few days it failed to respond to the application of mud packs, charms, and fetishes, Martin's wife was sore afraid. Villagers were nonplused and the condition became known as Martin Knee.

And so it happened that at length a grizzled trader chanced upon the village and, in due course, learned of the baffling Martin Knee malady. Pledging his help, and drawing upon his memory of an old Indian remedy, he concocted a potion derived from distilling rye mash in a pot still with juniper berries, grapes and aromatic herbs.

As Thomas patted the resulting mixture onto the inflamed knee, he licked his finger and was amazed to discover that it possessed a most interesting and pleasing taste. Taking a small sip, he found it not only pleasing, but warming to the gullet and stomach. Several more swallows brought home the realization that the pain in his knee had nearly vanished.

Word spread through the village that the Martin Knee was cured, and the recipe for the potion was quickly passed among the populace.

So overwhelmingly favorable was the reaction to the mixture, that an epidemic of Martin Knee ensued. Flimsy scaffolds were hastily constructed from which the townsfolk fortuitously fell, resulting in a rash of Martin Knee.

61

So widespread was the affliction, that the malady and the medication became synonymous, and a part of the village vocabulary, as in "I'll have another Martin Knee," or "There's nothing like a Martin Knee to ameliorate the vicissitudes of the day."

The origin of the Martini

62

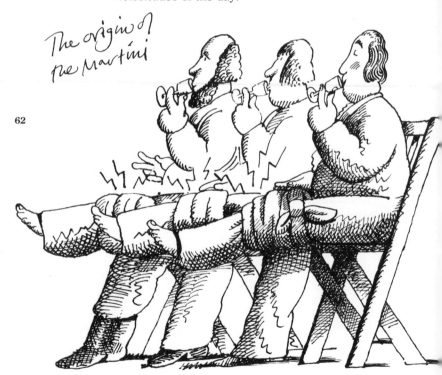

In time, of course, perversion of the language reduced Martin Knee to Martini.

Meanwhile, Thomas Martin's village became a center for the halt and the lame.

But nobody cared.

—Philip R. Emmons, Hillside, Ill.

Recipe for the Driest Martini
"The McGraw Masher *Extremely* Dry Martini": Pour 2 oz. of vodka into a tumbler over ice. Add a green olive. Drink while *looking at* a bottle of vermouth. Tasty.

—from INSTITUTIONS magazine, April 1, 1980

ADY CURZON SOUP

Every country has its specialties. In Germany, Lady Curzon Soup is on the top of the list, and it's a "must" on every restaurant's menu with a certain amount of pretention. A special cup—a little bit bigger than a demitasse cup and smaller than a teacup—was even designed for it and has become a standard item in restaurant china lines.

What is Lady Curzon Soup? Essentially it's a turtle soup with cream and sherry mixed into it.

Who was Lady Curzon? It took me quite a while to track her down. Her husband was Lord Curzon, Viceroy of India at the beginning of the century.

The story is that at a dinner in 1905 the guest of honor could not drink alcohol, so in order to include sherry in some form on the menu (at the time, no civilized Englishman would dine without it), Lady Curzon ordered the chef to put sherry in the turtle soup.

And some people have to discover a new continent to be remembered by history . . .

AESAR'S SALAD

Nobody agrees on who created the soufflé, Champagne, or the most famous salad of them all, Caesar's. Of the many alleged parents of the latter dish, only Alex Cardini is willing to bet $10,000 and a good bowl of Caesar's Salad to protect his claim as the originator.

Alex, born in 1899, began his restaurant apprenticeship in Italy at the age of ten, and by 1914 was working in London. He was called back to Italy to serve a five-year tour of duty as a pilot during World War I. Upon his discharge, he decided to join his brother, Caesar, who was proprietor of a restaurant in Tijuana, Mexico.

In 1927, Alex created a salad he called "Aviator's Salad" to honor fliers at nearby Rockwell Field in San Diego, California. With the quick popularity of the dish, it soon took on the more personal family name of "Caesar" and henceforth has been known as such.

HICKEN À LA KING

You would surely be puzzled reading "Chicken à la Keene" on a menu, yet that's what Chicken à la King was originally called. Claridge's of London insists that *their* chef created this dish to honor Mr. J. R. Keene, whose horse won the Grand Prix in 1881. But Charles Ranhofer, who was the chef of the original Delmonico's of New York (and published his monumental book *The Epicurean* in 1894), claimed that *he* invented it for the same family. When and why it was changed to "à la king" is one of the minor and not very exciting mysteries of culinary life.

65

UTLET POJARKSY

Cutlet Pojarksy is the dish that helps cut food costs in many restaurants. When ground veal or chicken is shaped in the form of a veal cutlet, coated with bread crumbs, and sautéed golden brown, it uncannily resembles the real thing. According to one of the more popular apocryphal stories, the Russian Czar stopped on the road between Saint Petersburg and Moscow at Pojarsky's Tavern. He demanded veal chops. The frightened tavern keeper produced one from scraps of meat to avoid eternal life in Siberia. The Czar liked it so much that . . . (you may finish the story without me).

 ## UCK MONTMORENCY

The second most popular duck preparation after *à l'orange* is not named after a great chef, a losing battle, or a character in a nineteenth-century play. The name originates from the village of Montmorency near Paris, where some of the finest cherries of France grow. The first time it was served was at the court of Henri IV.

 ## ILET DE SOLE MARGUERY

George Rector's father started Rector's, the restaurant which was "the center of all the population worth knowing," especially if your world was located somewhere between Wall Street and Broadway in New York in the Gay Nineties. Rector's was frequented by sports champions, opera stars, explorers, captains of industry and lieutenants of sloth, gamblers, adventurers, authors—and Diamond Jim Brady, first and foremost, together with his bodyguard (who had an eternally tanned face, doubtless from continued exposure to Diamond Jim's jewels).

Diamond Jim had been to Paris and had fallen in love with a dish called Filet de Sole Marguery, created by the chef-patron of the famed Parisian café-restaurant of the same name.

George was sent off to Paris to apprentice there and come back with the recipe or else.

After two arduous months, our George triumphantly landed back in New York's harbor, where he was greeted by Rector's Russian orchestra. That evening, Sam Shubert, Marshall Field, John Philip Sousa, and of course Diamond Jim Brady honored young George with a welcome banquet. Jim declared of the prized Marguery sauce: "It's so good I could eat it on a Turkish towel!"

When Diamond Jim passed away, Rector said sadly after the funeral. "I've lost my best four customers . . ."

Here is the recipe as it appeared in one of Rector's books, *The Girl from Rector's*, in 1927.

⦀ Filet de Sole Marguery
First, you must use none but imported sole from the

English Channel, which must be shipped over alive in tanks. Cut the fillet with a very sharp knife. There are four fillets to a fish. Take the rest of the fish and put them into a big boiler with plenty of leeks, onions, carrots, turnips, lettuce, romaine, parsley, and similar vegetables. The whole mass is reduced by boiling from eight to twelve hours. This leaves a very small quantity of a jellylike substance, which is the essence of the fish. If properly prepared, only a handful of jelly will be obtained from two hundred fish.

In another pan we place the yolks of four dozen eggs. Work a gallon of melted butter into this, stopping every ten minutes to pour in a pint of dry, white wine of good Bordeaux quality. Add from time to time a spoonful of the essence of fish. This is stirred in and cooked in a double boiler in the same way as you would make a hollandaise sauce.

Strain the sauce through a very fine sieve. Season with a dash of cayenne and salt. At no time in the preparation of the sauce should it be allowed to come to a boil.

Now we take the fillets, which should be kept on ice to retain their freshness until the sauce is ready. Place them in a pan with just sufficient water to float them a little. About half an inch of water should be sufficient to cover them. After they simmer for ten minutes or less remove and place on a silver platter. Garnish the dish on one end with small shrimp and on the other end with imported mussels from northern France.

Pour a liberal amount of the sauce over the whole platter. Sprinkle with chopped parsley and place under the grill for the purpose of allowing it to glaze to a golden brown. Then serve.

OMPANO EN PAPILLOTE

Pompano, one of the finest fish of North America, is abundant from North Carolina to Florida and in the Gulf of Mexico. The silvery fish weighing one and a half to two pounds is perhaps best simply broiled over charcoal, but the most famous preparation is *en papillote*, baked in buttered white butcher's paper.

69

Originally Mr. Jules Alciatore, founder of Antoine's restaurant in New Orleans, created this dish to honor the Montgolfier brothers, who had invented the world's first balloon in 1783. (When the fish is baked in the parchment paper, the heat puffs it up like a balloon.) Later, in the early 1900s, the famous Brazilian balloonist and flier, Alberto Santos-Dumont, displayed his stunts over New Orleans and the dish was served again, this time at a banquet honoring the balloonist. Now it has become part of the international culinary repertory, with sea trout, striped bass, or other similar fish sometimes substituting for pompano.

OURNEDOS ROSSINI

Rossini, the Italian composer, considered himself to be every bit as good a cook as a composer. He invented many dishes and spent most of the money he earned on trying to invent a new type of machine capable of making macaroni. A typical conversation of his was reported by one of his contemporaries:

> ROSSINI: How boring fame is! The pork butchers are the happy fellows.
> FRIEND: You should have been one.
> ROSSINI: Of course, I would have liked that . . . but as a youth I was so ill-advised!

Happily, he is just as famous for his Tournedos Rossini as he is for his *Barber of Seville*. Apparently one evening he was sitting at his favorite table at the Café Anglais, one of the most famous restaurants of the day, when, looking at the menu, he declared he was tired of every beef dish on it. When the maître-d'hôtel suggested a variety of other choices, Rossini brushed them aside, declaring that he liked only beef. Suddenly he looked with intensity toward the maître-d' and asked him to fry a crosscut of beef tenderloin in butter and place it on top of a fried crust, topping it with a slice of seasoned goose liver, again topped with "a fine slice of fresh truffle."

The startled restaurateur protested that he could not offer such a dish—it was unpresentable.

"Well, then arrange not to let it be seen."

The dish was prepared, served, and became an instant sensation. However, it was always prepared behind the guest's back. That's how apparently the name became *tourne le dos* (turn the back).

ALLY LUNN

When you mix milk, yeast, butter, sugar, eggs, flour, and a bit of salt, put the mixture into a tube pan, let it rise, and bake it, you do get a very nice sweet bread, but not so special that most every American cookbook would feature it since the mid-nineteenth century.

Unless, of course, its name was the kind that sticks in people's minds.

The bread I described is of French origin; it used to be sold on the streets of Paris by vendors who would cry: *"Sol et lune!!"* —referring to the golden brown top of the cake (the sun) and the almost white bottom (the moon). French emigrants brought it to the States and in time *sol et lune* became Americanized to "Sally Lunn." Today it is considered to be one of the most classic American breads.

If you don't care for the above explanation, I offer you another popular version: Sally Lunn cake is named after a woman who sold it in Bath, England, at the end of the eighteenth century. One night while hawking it on the street, she met a gentleman named Professor Higgins . . .

TRAWBERRIES ROMANOFF

Perhaps the greatest chef of them all, Carême, while working for Czar Alexander I of Russia, created Strawberries Romanoff (even if the late Mike Romanoff of Hollywood claimed he invented the dessert). According to the original recipe, very ripe strawberries were crushed and a crystal bowl was half filled with them. A good red Port wine was poured over the strawberries and, after this heavenly liquid was stirred, the bowl was placed in a cool spot overnight. The next day, the mixture was forced through a sieve and poured over fresh strawberries.

NDIANER

In the beginning of the nineteenth century, quite a few Hungarian aristocrats lived in Vienna, and some of them supported the arts as a hobby. Count Pálffy, for example, purchased the Theater an der Wien. Unfortunately, it was not a success; to make it more popular, the good count added various juggling acts to the musical operetta playing at the theater. One of the acts was an Indian chief who was a master of the blowgun. Apparently even this eighth wonder of the world didn't bring in the paying customers, and so Count Pálffy requested his pastry chef to invent a specialty that the ushers could pass out free as a kind of inducement. Although the name of this Hungarian chef is lost, he should be remembered because he created a kind of a whimsical takeoff on the face of the Indian (a chocolate bun with snow-white whipped-cream center), thus writing a new chapter in the art of pastry making, using whipped cream for the first time as part of a dessert.

By the following day the fame of this new delicacy had spread, and every pastry shop imitated it with more or less success, dubbing it "Indianer." Customers now stood in line with considerably more enthusiasm to get in to the aforementioned theater.

73

The year was 1831 and it was a memorable year if for no other reason than that *The Hunchback of Notre Dame* was published, and the Indianer, or *Mohrenkopf*, or "Indian doughnut" was served for the first time. Today there isn't a pastry shop-*Konditorei* in Vienna or in Budapest that doesn't serve this delightful delicacy.

 ## SKIMO PIE

If in the year 1919 you went into a little candy store in Onawa, Iowa, and ordered an I-Scream Bar, you would have gotten a small chocolate-covered ice cream pop. Christian Nelson, the proprietor of this store, got a patent for it in 1921 and eventually became a partner with Russell Stover, who renamed it the Eskimo Pie. The rest—as they say in bad biographies—is history.

ABA AU RHUM

If one were to try to list the ten most popular desserts around the world, *Baba au Rhum* would in all likelihood be on this super-inventory. Where did it come from?

Stanislas Leszczyński, King of Poland from 1704 to 1709, was an amateur baker. He also loved to read the *1001 Arabian Nights*. One day he created a dessert, naming it "Ali Baba," after one of the characters in the book. Whether he made the cake-dough exactly as we make it today we aren't sure, but he definitely came up with the idea of soaking the cake in rum and setting it aflame, then dramatically bringing it into the darkened, royal dining room. The cake, according to description, was moist and full of little bits of candied fruits and raisins.

After Stanislas was ousted by King Augustus, he found himself a pauper, exiled in France. His daughter, an uncommonly handsome lass, became the wife of Louis XV, which put our likable amateur gourmet, Stanislas, back into power and luxury. He became an amateur architect and designed an exquisite château in Nancy, where he gave some of the most talked-about parties, creating further masterpieces. Unfortunately, none of the other dishes has remained, but *Baba au Rhum* should be enough of a monument for even an ex-king.

The famous Parisian mâitre-pâtissier, Julienne, kept the cake base but changed the syrup, renaming it *Brillat-Savarin*, after the famous French gastronomist, and eventually it became known as a *Savarin*. That is why you'll find both names on today's menus.

YLLABUB UNDER THE COW

Elizabeth Raffald was one of the most remarkable ladies of all time: housekeeper to Lady Warburton; a midwife who organized the first Midwife's Guild; founder of a magazine called the *Manchester Guardian* (not the same as today's); author of the most popular cookbook of the eighteenth century (*The Experienced English Housekeeper*, first published in 1769); and, at the same time, mother of fifteen children in eighteen years of marriage. And she lived only forty-eight years!

She also managed to write the only recipe that calls for an "under the cow" version of syllabub, the most popular English drink, dating back to Elizabethan times. The name comes from *Sillery*, a section of Champagne country, and *bub*, which was Elizabethan slang for a drink that had bubbles in it.

To Make a Syllabub under the Cow

Put a bottle of strong beer and a pint of cyder into a punch bowl, grate in a small nutmeg, and sweeten it to your taste; then milk as much milk from the cow as will make a strong froth, and the ale look clear, let it stand an hour, then strew over it a few currants, well washed, picked and plumbed before the fire, then send it to the table.

77

ARL GREY'S TEA

England was always known for merchants who catered to the peculiar whims and tastes of the upper class. A shop specializing in the finest teas, George Charlton (at 48 Charing Cross) prepared a special blend of tea for the famous politician-statesman, Earl Grey. Eventually, with the Earl's permission, it was sold to the public in 1836, and a few years later, Robert Jackson & Company (at 1717 Piccadilly until last year when it closed) bought the secret formula for the blending of the tea.

BONES on the TABLE:
NOTES ABOUT TABLE MANNERS

CHAPTER

4

HINESE TABLE MANNERS FROM A TO B

The first time I heard the phrase "table manners," was during a luncheon when I was about six. My mother coolly informed me that eating soup so that people could hear me clearly in the next town was not "proper table manners."

How shocked I was some thirty years later when a Chinese friend of mine cheerfully told me, when I was dining in his home, that *not* smacking one's lips while eating or slurping the soup if it's delicious (to prolong the pleasure) is foolish. Only Westerners, whose culinary development was arrested a long time ago, would make rules otherwise, he observed.

Chinese society considers table manners extremely important, and if you aren't mindful, you will be considered a *fan-kwey*, a foreign devil, and never be invited again.

cultural misunderstanding

To prevent such an unfortunate happening, I will jot down a few rules, regulations, formalities, and customs generally expected in polite Chinese society. It is a compilation of friends' stories told during delicious dinners in Hong Kong, Taiwan, Canton, New York, and other places; the puckish advice of Lin Yu Tang; the wisdom of my taxi driver in the New Territories near Hong Kong; and notes from learned books like *The Musings of a Gourmet* by F. T. Cheng, *The Secrets of Chinese Cooking* by Mrs. C. T. Wang, and others.

Seating

Chinese emperors were honored as the Sons of Heaven and, as such, their throne was always placed on the north side of the throne room facing southward. Tradition dictates that you must seat your guest of honor on the north side of the table facing south and you, as a host, must sit opposite the guest of honor and not next to him or her. Oriental logic dictates that the opposite of the honored place would be the least important seat at the table and you as the host should sit there.

However, in Canton, the guest of honor is seated to the left of the host, two seats away, and the next in importance sits in a corresponding chair on the right side.

Tea

The host usually will offer the cup in both hands and you must rise from your seat and receive it the same way.

Either to indicate that you would like to have tea or that

you have enough in your cup, or to thank someone for pouring tea, you should tap the table with stretched out forefinger to signify "kowtow."

Wash your teacup in a bowl of tea before drinking from it in a restaurant.

If you're in a restaurant and would like to have your teapot refilled, remove the lid from the pot.

Manners

Eat from your side of the common platter only.

It is permissible to put bones directly on the table.

To be loud, laugh heartily, and tell stories in a stentorian voice is perfectly acceptable.

Do not spread out the rice to cool.

Never add condiments to the common platter or soup bowl.

Everyone eats with the right hand. Even left-handed children are taught to hold the chopsticks with the right hand.

Some fish, like garoupa, are difficult to eat because the meat sticks to the bones. When the top half is finished, it should be turned over in order to make it easier to eat.

Since boatmen are always afraid of their boat turning over and capsizing, when someone turns over fish, he will automatically say "the boat next to mine."

Put one large spoonful and one small scoop of rice into your individual bowl: the large one is for yourself and the small one is for the gods.

In China, clarity of wine has always been important; in the nineteenth century, a standard line on invitations was: "We have polished our wineglasses for this occasion already." In extremely polite families, this line is still used.

 ## OOK MA, ALL HANDS!

My friend Craig Claiborne, senior food critic of the *New York Times*, insists on sizzling hot food on a sizzling hot platter (even though it may ruin the sauce). But he's not the first. The ancient Greeks were addicted to the hottest possible temperature in foods as well.

Unfortunately, since they ate with their fingers, this caused some problems on occasion. Ancient Greek gourmets were known to train their fingers and hands to withstand extraordinary heat by dipping them daily into hotter and hotter liquid. So when the food was put in the center of the table these finger-trained gentlemen could plunge into the goodies before anyone else could possibly touch it.

They tried to be very neat about it but since most of the foods were sauced casseroles, by the third or fourth dish their clothing reflected the menu. Thus it became a part of the ancient Greek etiquette to change clothes between courses.

85

Neither Romans nor Greeks knew napkins, but Romans used a *mappa*, a sort of linen bag which the guest brought with him to wipe his mouth with and, if he liked some dish particularly, he put it into the bag and brought it home.

By the time of the Renaissance, linen runners were put on top of the table, and the ends were used by the guests to tidy up.

In Elizabethan times the napkin was tied around the neck, to save the lovely starched white ruffles. It was not, however, an easy matter to knot the two ends together, and this is where the expression "to make both ends meet" originates.

HIRTEENTH-CENTURY ETIQUETTE

The following notes are taken from Fra Bonvesin's *Fifty Courtesies of the Table* (Ambrosian Library at Milan), a set of fifty rhymed maxims or "courtesies."

It is to the extreme gluttonous and vile, and showing great contempt of the Lord, to think of eating before having asked His blessing.

Do not fill your mouth too full; the glutton who fills his mouth will not be able to reply when spoken to.

When thirsty, swallow your food before drinking.

Do not dirty the cup in drinking; take it with both hands firmly, so as not to spill the wine. If not wishing to drink, and your neighbor has dirtied the cup, wipe it before passing it on.

Those taking soup, do not swallow your spoons.

Do not soak your bread in your wine.

Always remember if a friend be dining with one, to help him to the choicest parts. Do not, however, press your friend too warmly to eat or drink, but receive him well, and give him good cheer.

Let those who serve be clean, and let the servants be free from any smell which might give a nausea to those eating.

Let the hands be clean, and above all do not at table scratch your head, nor indeed any portion of your body.

When eating with others, do not sheath your knife before everyone else at the table has done the same.

Do not mix together on your plate all sorts of viands, meat, and eggs, for it may disgust your neighbor.

87

HEN HOW DID SHE GET TO BE A SIZE 18?

In Victorian England, if a young lady wanted to be considered properly spiritual, dainty, and refined, she could not be caught visibly enjoying food or wine. To prevent this, she usually ate heartily in her room before coming down to join others in the dining room.

In medieval India, women did the same but for different reasons. Since male guests were supposed to have the best morsels, the ladies had a pre-meal in their apartments to be able to withstand the temptation.

ORN AGAIN

On June 24, 1774, the National Convention of the French Revolution had summoned up the courage to denounce and arrest Robespierre who, down but by no means out, was hustled off to prison. At this moment, during a most dangerous and significant coup d'état, with the situation touch and go, the Convention declared a two-hour recess for dinner, since the time was 5:00 in the afternoon. A Frenchman does not willingly tolerate an intrusion on the hour he dines.

ASHINGTON, D.C., THE BEAUTIFUL

John Adams, John Tyler, Franklin Pierce, Theodore Roosevelt (in 1901), Woodrow Wilson, Calvin Coolidge, Harry Truman (in 1945) had one Inaugural Ball; William Henry Harrison in 1841, Zachary Taylor in 1849, and Harry Truman in 1949 had three, and Dwight Eisenhower in 1957 had four, the most ever.

The wildest one was Zachary Taylor's, where at a midnight buffet all good manners were abandoned. People gorged themselves until 4 A.M., threw turkey legs, dug their hands into cakes, and women screamed and fainted.

The most elaborate one was probably Ulysses S. Grant's second inauguration on March 4, 1873, which even had fireworks all evening, costing $40,000. The ball was held in a 350 × 110-foot temporary building in Judiciary Square, but they forgot to supply heat and everybody was forced to keep their coats on. For the $20 ante you could partake in the buffet which consisted of:

10,000 fried oysters
8,000 scalloped oysters
8,000 pickled oysters
63 boned turkeys,
    12 pounds each
15 saddles of mutton
40 pieces of spiced beef,
    40 pounds each
200 dozen roasted quails
100 game pâtés,
    50 pounds each
300 tongues
200 hams, ornamented
    with jelly
30 baked salmon
100 chickens
400 partridges
25 stuffed boars' heads
40 pâtés de foie gras,
    10 pounds each
20,000 headcheese
    sandwiches
3,000 ham sandwiches
3,000 beef-tongue
    sandwiches
1,600 celery bunches
30 barrels of salad

2 barrels of lettuce
350 chickens boiled for salad
6,000 eggs boiled for salad
1 barrel of beets
2,500 loaves of bread
8,000 rolls
24 cases of Prince Albert
    crackers
1,000 pounds of butter
300 Charlotte Russes,
    17 pounds each
200 molds of wine jelly
200 molds of blancmange
300 gallons of ice cream
200 gallons of flavored ices
400 pounds of pastry
150 large decorated cakes
60 large pyramid cakes
25 barrels of Málaga grapes
15 cases of oranges
5 cases of apples
400 pounds mixed candies
10 cases of raisins
200 pounds shelled almonds
500 gallons of claret punch
300 gallons of coffee
200 gallons of tea
100 gallons of chocolate

BUT NO HEAT!

Everybody ignored the magnificent cold buffet and rushed for the hot coffee. Next day the papers reported: "Those assembled were frozen out before midnight."

Whatever Happened
TO
ESCOFFIER?
AND
OTHER STORIES
ABOUT CHEFS

CHAPTER
5

Escoffier
rejecting
souffles

PROMISE HER ANYTHING BUT GIVE HER PARTRIDGE À L'ARPEGE

Escoffier was chef of the Carlton Hotel in London for fifteen years. Long before World War I his salary was £2,000 a year, a goodly sum in those days. He invented some of our richest and most complicated dishes, but he himself ate very little meat and only one real meal a day. "Generally speaking," he said, "a cook's senses—his mind, eyes, ears, palate—are full of the smell of food. It is seldom he decides to eat any of his creations, he has spent all his enthusiasm on their preparation. I like simple dishes like potatoes boiled in water and simple vegetables."

Yet when a Brazilian millionaire ordered partridge *à l'eau de cologne* (during his days at the London Carlton), Escoffier undertook its preparation. The only thing he asked was which brand of cologne should be used in the sauce!

Another time, an American tycoon, famous for his stinginess, asked Escoffier in Monte Carlo to prepare for him a menu which would offer the most expensive dishes ever served, within a fabulous repast for twelve. Escoffier then started serious research and succeeded in creating twenty dishes which cost several thousand dollars each—the rarest game, birds, exotic animals, their eyes to be replaced by pearls and diamonds, and Champagne pouring from golden fountains in the center of the tables. Proudly he presented the proposed bill of fare to the tycoon, who was most impressed and said, "Okay, I need at least a dozen copies—of course, charge me for your time and trouble." When Escoffier's eyes formed big question marks, he answered, "I only want the menus, not the food. I want to send them to my friends in America to show them what wonderful meals I have had in Europe."

Once, when Escoffier did not know the exact timing of a dinner (because of the many courses involved and also because of speeches and other extenuating circumstances), he made ten different batches of soufflés, starting three minutes apart, to assure that one would be ready at just the right moment. The others were thrown out.

94

THER THAN THAT, MME VATEL, HOW DID YOU LIKE THE FISH COURSE?

Everybody eats; many are fascinated by the art of cooking; a few dabble in its mysteries. Louis XIII was an excellent pâtisseur, Louis XV brewed his own coffee, and Frederick the Great and Kant both enjoyed creating their own menus.

Every nation has produced ten good poets for every good cook; this must have been clear to the ancient Greeks too, because cooks were not slaves but gentlemen and free citizens. They had to be courted and coaxed, particularly if they were artists of the stature of one Martialis mentions, who cooked a whole meal using nothing but squash. Among the Sybarites, cooks insisted their employers send out invitations a year ahead.

Although in Rome chefs were slaves, they were so expensive that Pliny remarked that a good cook cost more than a victory parade. Mark Antony gave a whole town to his chef after a particularly successful banquet, as a token of appreciation. On the other hand, when a meal was unsuccessful, public spankings of cooks were common. Or worse, the unfortunate cook might be sold off, together with other slaves.

Sixteenth-century Italy and seventeenth-century France produced more inventive chefs than the rest of the world the rest of the time. (Nineteenth-century France, of course, had virtually dozens of great chefs, but they mainly enlarged upon and defined the achievements of their predecessors.) During this golden era in France it was permissible among the aristocracy to steal lovers or mistresses, but an unforgivable crime to purloin a rival's chef.

Small wonder that all over the civilized world cooks felt they ought to be honored, and were. Even Frederick the Great, whose cook delighted him with a new ragout, expressed his thanks in a poetic epistle.

The professional chefs' society, to which I used to belong as a practicing cook, was named after one of the true martyrs of cooking—Vatel, who fell on his own sword when the Dover sole he had ordered for a royal dinner failed to arrive on time because of a storm in the English Channel. Escoffier was asked by an English reporter whether he too would have committed suicide in such a case, to which he replied, "No, I would have made a mousse of young chicken breasts and covered it with a fish velouté, and nobody would have known the difference . . .!"

96

WHAT'S A KITCHINER, ANYWAY?

Every now and then there is an unclassifiable gifted person who baffles encyclopedists and other intellectual bureaucrats. Dr. Kitchiner is a fine example: he was a nonpracticing London physician with a burning interest in cooking, optics, music, and travel. He wrote several books, among them *Practical Observations on Telescopes, Opera-Glasses and Spectacles* (1815), *The Economy of the Eyes* (1824), and one of the first guidebooks: *The Traveller's Oracle and Horse and Carriage Keeper's Guide*. As a musician he edited many songs and wrote dozens of others.

He became a household word when in 1817 he published his classic work *The Cook's Oracle* and later *The Housekeeper's Oracle*—associating the science of nutrition with the refinements of the art of cookery and the amenities of the table.

97

Once weekly, he held a party called a *conversazione* at his house. When guests entered the first thing they saw was a big sign: "Come at seven—Go at eleven." Dinner was served at 9:30 sharp, and precisely at eleven, hats and coats were brought in by servants, and Dr. Kitchiner bade good-night to his guests.

If the invitation was for 7:00 you had better have been there because five minutes later the door was locked. Dr. Kitchiner mentioned in one of his invitations:

> To insure the punctual attendance of those illustrious gastrophilists who on grand occasions are invited to join this high tribunal of taste for their own pleasure and the benefit of their country, it is irrevocably resolved, that the janitor be ordered not to admit any visitor, of whatever eminence of appetite, after the hour at which the Secretary shall have announced that the Specimens are ready.

AKED CAME THE PIGEON

Alexis Soyer was the most fascinating and many-sided chef of the last two centuries. He was born in 1809 in France and eventually became chef of the famous Reform Club in London. Among his many achievements is the creation of the professional modern kitchen as we know it today; five major books in gastronomic literature; and military service with the British forces in the Crimean War, working alongside Florence Nightingale. He died in 1858 at the age of forty-nine. Contemporaries describe him as someone who was eccentric to the point of being ridiculous. He dressed in colorful costumes in an age known for drab garb, organized soup kitchens for the poor, and at the same time spent money extravagantly on his friends.

Once he was competing in the town of Slough, west of London, against five other chefs (including two from the

Royal Household and the chef of Baroness Rothschild) to create "the most novel dish which is as light as possible."

Soyer's entry, "La Croustade Sylphe en Surprise à la Cerito" was carried in. When the lid was removed, a beautiful pigeon flew out the window and off toward London. (This was certainly lighter than air.) Under the dish where the pigeon had been was the entire dinner:

A dish both light and novel

Salade Composée of Filets of Grouse à la Bohémienne, Côtelettes of Veal and Mushrooms, and beneath that the dessert, Crème aux Pêches.

Soyer had made a bet with some friends in London that he would send part of his dish from Slough so fast that only the electric telegraph could get it to London faster. His friends in London were telegrammed when the dish was placed on the table and twenty-four minutes later, the pigeon flew in bearing the message under its wing: "Please pay the *chef de cuisine* of the Reform Club the sum of fifty pounds, for my private apartment in his new dish."

Once Soyer fell through the ice in St. James's Park and was saved from drowning by the Royal Humane Society's iceman. To express his gratitude, he sent the society a subscription of ten guineas together with a sketch of a device he invented for retrieving immersed ice skaters. This was followed by a dinner at the Freemasons' Tavern, after which Soyer led a parade of rescued persons.

S DANTE SAID, "GIVE 'EM HELL, CHEF"

In a delightful book published in 1903, *Millionaire Households and Their Domestic Economy*, a lady named Mary Elizabeth Carter discusses the character and role of the "proper" chef among other matters of decorum and etiquette for the wealthy set. When I read the following, I was sure Mrs. Carter was describing some of the chefs I have encountered in various hotels and restaurants around the world.

> The chef can snub with a shoulder shrug, wilt with one glance of his expressive eyes; or, when excited to anger, annihilate by an avalanche of scornful words. Then again he is childlike in his *naïveté*—bland as the "heathen Chinee." We never know what to expect of him.

> No one would have the temerity to interfere or dictate to him. Usually he is not seen in costume beyond the kitchen, but now and then he may be summoned above stairs to an audience with "Madame." When this uncommon event occurs, he dons a fresh white suit and appears, cap in hand, at the door of the dainty boudoir.

> If he speaks with but little English, they will hang upon his words and watch his expressive pantomime in order to do his bidding, as well as to keep *en rapport* with his rapid movements.

101

Many chefs I've known could easily buy and sell the restaurant they work for. Some of their income still comes (seventy-seven years after this book was written) from what is called in the vernacular "kickbacks":

Woe betide the luckless butcher, fishmonger, or green-grocer, who unwarily refuses to give our chef commissions. He will soon find that his goods are unsatisfactory, and lose the custom of that house.

On the whole, however, the chef's life-style has changed considerably since 1906:

As a matter of course Chef lives high, is rosy, rotund, and comfortable. Later in life he will probably follow in the footsteps of epicures and become gouty or dyspeptic.

 ## HE RULES OF THE CHEF

1. The Chef is right.
2. The Chef is always right.
3. The Chef does not sleep, he rests.
4. The Chef doesn't eat, he nourishes himself.
5. The Chef doesn't drink, he tastes.
6. The Chef is never late, he is delayed.
7. The Chef never leaves the service, he is called away.
8. If you enter the Chef's office with your own idea, you leave with his.
9. The Chef doesn't have a relationship with his secretary, he educates her.
10. It is forbidden for Chefs to marry in order that their numbers shouldn't increase.
11. The Chef is always the Chef, even in his swimming costume.
12. If you criticize the Chef, you criticize the Almighty.

—found on the bulletin board of the Chef's Office aboard the QUEEN ELIZABETH II.

very funny
very funny

ELEPHANT
SCHNITZEL
AND OTHER
STRANGE
DELICACIES

CHAPTER
6

TRY THE KANGAROO CUTLET INSTEAD?

In some parts of Africa, the base of the elephant's trunk is considered to be one of the greatest delicacies; the cheeks and feet are also very desirable parts; the marrow of the leg bones eaten raw is a sovereign remedy for women's infertility as well as anybody's pain in the belly. The elephant's heart roasted on a forked stick over embers and served with rice is "fit for a king." (I understand that an elephant's heart can weigh more than sixty pounds and measure five feet in circumference.)

Paul Corcellet, who opened his famous gourmet shop in Paris in 1933, became instantly known as the man who cooked not only Elephant's Trunk, but also Lion's Steak, Giraffe's Neck, and other delicacies in traditional French style. He was also among the first to use flash-freezing in France.

He ruined forever, however, the punchline of the great story about a restaurant in Vienna that advertised it would serve absolutely any dish a guest requested. The first guest requested an elephant schnitzel. The waiter called the owner, who informed the guest: "I'm sorry, sir, but we can't cut up a whole elephant for a single schnitzel." Monsieur Corcellet does.

RODENT OF ANOTHER COLOR

Just in case you find some ostrich meat in your local supermarket, I share with you a recipe for it. I found it in a book attributed to the Roman gourmet Apicius, who squandered most of his large fortune on extravagant feasts in the first century A.D.

Boiled Ostrich

A stock in which to cook ostrich: pepper, mint, cumin, leeks, celery seed, dates, honey, vinegar, raisin wine, broth, a little oil.

Boil this in the stock kettle with the ostrich. Remove the bird when done and strain the liquid. Thicken with roux. Add the ostrich meat cut in convenient pieces, sprinkle with pepper. If you wish it more seasoned or tasty, add garlic while cooking ostrich.

And here is the oft-talked about, but rarely published, recipe for preparing a nice, fat, juicy dormouse.

Stuffed Dormouse

The animal is stuffed with a forcemeat of pork and small pieces of dormouse meat trimmings, all pounded with pepper, nuts and broth. Put the dormouse thus stuffed in an earthenware casserole, roast it in the oven, or boil it in the stock pot.

The ancient Romans prized dormice and used to fatten

them in the dark in specially made containers. They were then weighed at the table as a show of hospitality. (A nicely rounded arboreal rodent is the size of a well-developed rat.)

OO FOOD

Much has been written about the cold and endless winter of 1870–1871 during which Paris was besieged by the Prussians and the

107

Paris Zoo sold its animals to the butchers. French culinary genius was necessary to transform the local rodents into exquisite ragouts and casseroles, and the great chefs did not let the local gourmets down. In the Hôtel Place de la Ville there was a daily rat market, and one restaurant in particular featured them cooked with truffles and champagne.

According to contemporary records recipes were also exchanged for transforming prized poodles or common mongrels into dainty dinners.

108

HOU SHALT EAT ONLY KOSHER GRASSHOPPERS

In different parts of the world, people happily couple *foie gras* with truffles, pasta with cheese, or cream cheese and lox with bagels. In the Bible a specialty dish was locust with honey, however unappetizing that combination may seem today. The Orthodox Jewish laws specifically permit the eating of grasshoppers and various sorts of locusts. Leviticus 11:22 reads: "Of these you may eat the following: the common locust in its several species, the flying locust in its several species, and the grasshopper in its several species."

In the Gospel according to Matthew, when John the Baptist preached in the wilderness of Judea, he "had his raiment of camel's hair and a leathern girdle about his loins; and his meat was locusts with wild honey."

Mohammed's wives used to send him trays of locusts as presents.

Man about to eat a Bit O' Locust candy bar

New Caledonians in the South Pacific are known to munch spiders happily while watching TV reruns in the village hall, and in Germany, a country always addicted to odd practices, boys devour the cockchafer-beetle alive, removing first its wings and legs.

There's a fascinating little book, *Why Not Eat Insects?* by Vincent M. Holt, written in 1885 in England. The author points out that the great majority of insects live entirely on vegetable matter while the lobster, "the creature consumed in such incredible quantities at all the highest tables in the land, is such a foul feeder that, for its sure capture the experienced will bait his lobster pot with putrid flesh of fish which is too far gone to even attract a crab."

110

He quotes the famous French scientist, René Réaumur, who knew of a young lady so fond of spiders that she never saw one without catching and eating it. Lelande, the French astronomer, had similar tastes; and Rosel speaks of a German who was in the habit of "spreading spiders, like butter on bread."

"What a godsend to housekeepers to discover a new entrée to vary the monotony of the present round! Curried Maychafers or perhaps Fried Chafers with Wireworm Sauce," Holt cries.

Speaking of caterpillars, he seems to read their little minds: "Does not the sweet scent of our cooked bodies

tempt you? Fry us with butter; we are delicious. Boil us,
grill us, stew us: we are good all ways!"

He suggests the following festive dinner menu:

Slug Soup
Fried Soles with Woodlouse Sauce
Wasp Grubs Fried in the Comb
Boiled Neck of Mutton with Wireworm Sauce
Braised Beef with Caterpillars
Gooseberry Cream with Sawflies
Stag Beetle Larvae on Toast

111

Just in case you are not partial to one of the above
delicacies, as an alternative he suggests the surefire Moths
on Toast.

HE ALTERNATIVE

When I first read Hector Bolitho's *The
Glorious Oyster* (New York: Horizon Press,
1960), I knew I could stop worrying about the

nutritional problems of cannibals. Wrote he, "Maoris used to eat each other before our ancestors arrived. We did not succeed in curing them of their primitive habits. Even these poor cannibals had more imagination in preparing their food than the people in the hotel."

Recently I learned that there are certain primitive tribes that practice *exocannibalism*, partaking of the flesh of enemies only. Unfortunately, there are still some misguided groups, associations, and corporations that practice endocannibalism and only eat their friends . . .

112

I guess that's where the old cliché comes from: "Familiarity breeds endocannibalism."

L'Elisir d'Amore:
APHRODISIAC
TRIVIA
CHAPTER
7

IN'T MISBEHAVING

In every society, as in every age, there has been an attempt to make the science of nutrition serve the art of love. Culinary aphrodisiacs share three things in common: (1) they have a large body of literature, (2) they evoke great faith on the part of desperate people, and (3) their supposed effects are based on very little scientifically controlled data.

Any dissertation on the subject of cuisine and love must take France as a point of departure. When Louis XIV began to have problems satisfying Mme de Maintenon, she concocted for him a cordial of distilled spirits, sugar, and orange water, infused with parfums. It would appear that she either encountered a resistant condition or believed that the patient needed combination therapy because she also created Côtelettes de Veau à la Maintenon, which included "restorative ingredients of anchovy, sweet basil, cloves, coriander, and brandy."

> Take one-inch thick cutlets, lard them with strips of anchovy, ham, and bacon. Place them in a casserole with onions, a bunch of parsley, scallions, laurel leaf, sweet basil, heads of cloves, and coriander. After slightly browning the cutlets in butter, they should be left to simmer over a slow fire in their own gravy and a few large spoonfulls of brandy.

Mme Du Barry, the famous mistress of Louis XV, relied instead on ginger soufflés.

Culinary aphrodisiacs were not restricted to the rich and famous. The streets of Paris have echoed through the ages with this cry of street vendors: "artichokes, artichokes . . . heat the body, the spirit and the genitals."

When the French writer Hector Dirssot sought to revive himself after lovemaking, he ate an eel dish with truffles, wrapped in buttered paper and charcoal-roasted. It was served on a bed of crayfish ragout spiced with cayenne. According to his anecdotal testimony, this was especially effective when accompanied by a good Sauternes wine. He held that the combined therapy served his purpose splendidly, but unfortunately corroborative data from the ladies was not recorded.

For French men or women who are allergic to seafood dishes, but still treasure some of the nation's great delicacies, similar effects have been attributed to the heavily scented white truffles of the Piemonte region of Italy, whose recognized aphrodisiac qualities were thought to be reinforced if lightly sautéed with goose liver and a bit of white wine.

A significant literature is available on the subject because truffles were considered great passion builders. In fact, famous gastronome Brillat-Savarin, who in 1825 wrote a witty treatise on the art of dining called *La Physiologie du Goût*, reported that a French lady of solid virtue almost gave in to a handsome gourmet who fed her on truffled fowl from Périgueux. Anyone who loves good food can attest that when trying to diet, it is very difficult to remain virtuous when confronted with truffles from Périgueux, whether in *foie gras* or cooked in a fowl, or perhaps roasted whole in ashes.

It should be noted on the other side of the moral coin that famous Parisian brothels, some of them more luxuriously and tastefully decorated than society ladies' boudoirs, routinely served *le petit souper* for their customers. This was so strong a drawing card that the brothels competed furiously with each other for imaginative chefs who could concoct dishes reputed to be effective aphrodisiacs. According to hearsay, this is still common practice in Paris.

117

Since one cannot speak of French food without addressing
French wines, it should be noted that Vin de Gentiane
tastes fine and is reputed to be a generator of sexual
energy. Here is a recipe:

> Grate one ounce of gentian root and let it soak for a day
> in 3½ pints of good Cognac. Add half a pint of Bordeaux
> wine, filter it through a fine sieve, and seal it. After the
> eighth day, get ready for a great night.

France, furthermore, may spare one a trip to Central
America in search of some of the more exotic aphrodisiacs.
Some of these call for such special ingredients as crocodile
kidneys, ground spiders, and the sexual organs of an
assortment of animals. Those in need can shop at the
aforementioned Parisian delicacy shop, Corcellet, for such
culinary exotica as tiger steaks, elephant foot, or crocodile
fillets.

If you are visiting Morocco and have the need, a number of
couscous recipes may serve. Some of the most delicious
are made with a mixture of many spices called
ras-el-hanout. Literally, *ras-el-hanout* means "best of
shop" and each household or food shop makes its own.
Among the herbs it contains which are reputed to conjure
up passion are Spanish Fly, ashberries, and monk's
peppers. It has been reported that the mere mention of this
mixture will put a gleam into a Moroccan's eye. If your
couscous does not work, you can at least have the

consolation that the concoction you're eating tastes delicious.

In China, whose cuisine has a multimillennial history, culinary aphrodisiacs were used more often than they were written about. While many of the formulas are shrouded in history, we do know that the ground horn of the rhinoceros was considered particularly efficacious, albeit horribly expensive. The matter of cost, however, rarely stood in the way of emperors in need.

On a less costly and more delectable note, bird's-nest soup, one of my gustatory favorites, is a dish that many aficionados consider to have good aphrodisiac qualities. Another aphrodisiac food in Southeast Asia is the Vietnamese *nuoc-man,* made with an extract from fermented fish and a standard sauce. We know not whether the mechanism of its action is the result of the concentrated phosphorus, in which fish spawn is extremely rich. Sea cucumber, ginger, bamboo shoots, fried chicken gizzard, golden dates steamed in a casserole with ham, and lobster with pickled bean-curd sauce are other Chinese culinary aphrodisiac prescriptions.

In the classical period, the ancient Greeks swore by the effectiveness of carrots and leeks. The combination preparation was called *philtron* and was taken freely to lengthen the sexual act. There have been distinctions between so-called philtres, concoctions of herbs which induce love toward a particular person—a remarkable example of specificity of action—and out-and-out aphrodisiacs of *poculum amatorium*, concoctions which induced a temporary and more generalized state of amorousness.

In considering the administration of aphrodisiacs, one should keep in mind that Lucullus died of a love potion given to him by a jealous servant. An effective aphrodisiac dose, if such there is, may be close to the toxic.

In the Middle Ages there was quite a range of good-tasting traditional love potions: marzipan made with rosewater, almonds and honey; a hippocras brew made of cinnamon, ginger, and vanilla buds mixed in rhubarb juice doesn't sound bad either. In those days vervain (verbena) also enjoyed vogue as an aphrodisiac, and one can draw one's own conclusion about the fact that it was also worn about the neck, if a person was bruised. There were at least 180 varieties of herbs with aphrodisiac properties in the medieval herbal pharmacopoeia, so you could take your pick of those that suited your specific needs.

Most of them contained sugar mixed with other ingredients, anything from esoteric plants to simple goat's milk. These could be cooked with rice mixed with sparrow eggs boiled in milk and ghee (clarified butter), honey, sugar and sesame seed, often fennel, and plants native to India and impossible for some of us to pronounce. The claims made for most of these were that if they were taken regularly, you would be able to "enjoy many women with sexual vigor."

Virtually every country on the continent in the Middle Ages considered myrtle as a restorative. An authentic Portuguese Rx, to which the English added spirit of musk and ambergris, was called A Curious Water of Myrtle Flowers:

Take the flowers and leaves of myrtle, two handfuls, infuse them in two quarts of spring water, and then distill them in a cold still. This will be of a strong scent and tincture, and by adding more or less of the myrtle you may make it stronger or weaker as you please. This beautifies, and mixed with cordial syrups is a good cordial and inclines those that drink it to be very amorous.

121

And here, perhaps, reference should be made to the medieval German duke Henry of Saxony (c. 1108–1139), who declared that coriander, violet, and valerian were mighty powerful aphrodisiacs, especially if picked in the last quarter of the moon; if even higher potency was desired, pistachio nuts, chestnuts, and satyrion could be added to the mixture. The saving grace of Henry of Saxony's prescription was that at least he suggested the mixture be boiled in muscatel wine.

Later we find that two of the herbs and spices most often associated with aphrodisiac power are cumin and basil. Cumin has been added to cakes as recently as the nineteenth century. Ladies gave such cakes to their lovers to "turn them on," and ate some themselves to enhance their sexual attraction.

In 1926 the Dutch gynecologist Van de Velde, in a classic book on sexual technique, discussed aphrodisiacs and attributed to crayfish soup the same qualities as Chinese bird's-nest soup. He also suggested that calf's brain, because it is high in lecithin, may have some effect.

In a recent report by a New York physician dealing with impotence and frigidity, the suggestion was made that eggs, oysters, caviar, saffron, pepper, and mustard have an "undoubted effect in stimulating the libido and the erection center." As to the erotic virtues of garlic, the doctor noted, "Many of our Anglo-Saxons perhaps prefer their impotence to the alternative of having to eat garlic."

BUT DOES IT WORK WITH WONDER BREAD?

In Suffolk, England, in the nineteenth century, the standard remedy for whooping cough was moldy bread. A piece of bread was wrapped in cloth, buried for several days, and then fed to the patient. If he survived the remedy, the whooping cough was gone too. Perhaps this was an early form of penicillin?

I'LL BET CLARENCE BIRDS-EYE NEVER HAD WARTS

If you happen to have a wart you want to get rid of, you might as well try the Cornish method. Take a nine-pea pod and rub the warts with it. Then throw it away and chant "Wart, wart, wart, fly away, fly away!"

I must record, however, that Pliny, in his *Natural History*, recommended touching each wart with a different pea, then wrapping the peas in a cloth and throwing them away over your shoulder. Please take note: the only time this is supposed to be effective is the very first day of the new moon, unfortunately.

AKE TWO ASPIRIN AND A BOWL OF LENTIL SOUP

In ancient times opinions varied widely on the benefits or ill effects of beans and lentils. Hippocrates spoke about them as "rough, creating gluey blood which stops up the liver, creates melancholia, fourth-day shivers, heavy dreams, and dulls the vision and the strength of the brain." Nevertheless, he admitted that mixed with vinegar, onion, parsley, capers, marjoram, rosemary, and other blood-thinning ingredients, well-greased and accompanied by a lot of bread—they made a most suitable dish for peasants.

Other philosophers felt differently and summarized the virtues of the wise man thus: "To do all good, and to prepare lentils wisely." Galen used the liquid of boiled

lentils for treatment of certain stomach disorders and smallpox.

Herodotus reported that in Egypt the priests sworn to celibacy were not even allowed to look at beans. Pythagoras forbade his pupils to consume beans, declaring that they disturbed the clarity of the mind.

Medieval doctors disagreed and found all kinds of chemical and medicinal virtues in beans and lentils and recommended them very highly for people in all walks of life.

129

 ## ALM FOR YOUR NERVES AND OTHER PARTS AS WELL

The Bible tells us that Solomon suggested his son eat honey because it ennobled the human spirit.

Hippocrates and other doctors in ancient times mixed honey with milk and administered it to patients with kidney trouble.

Democritus confessed that the secret of his health (he died at age one hundred nine) was applying "honey inside and oil outside." He requested that, in the style of the Babylonians, his body be conserved with honey. Pope Sylvester II, who died in 1003, was actually embalmed with honey by an Arabic expert sent from Spain.

The Romans as usual went overboard: they even dipped radish, garlic, or sauerkraut into honey. During the excavation of the sixth-century temple at Paestum near Naples, archeologists found an amphora, partially filled with honey, which was still in perfect condition.

Even beeswax was used in folk medicine. The diseased part of the body was shaped out of the beeswax and placed on the altar, while praying to the gods for help in curing the sickness.

130

HOPPING FOR SERPENT WINE IN CHINA

Walking into a general store in Kwangchow, I saw many familiar foods that I had seen in Chinese supermarkets all over Asia. But suddenly I found myself facing a shelf with endless rows of wines. The label on the back of the bottle of the first one I noticed explained that it contained viper meat in corn liquor. I'm fond of reading eighteenth-century European herbariums, but now I was looking at medicated tonics far more exotic than anything I'd ever read about. Thousands of years ago the famous Chinese physician Shen Nun (2737–2697 B.C.) discovered the effectiveness of herbal tonics in curing many physical and mental diseases, and variations of these tonics are still found in China today.

I purchased a bottle of this viper liquor called *San She Chiew*, together with the snake lying in a state of stupor on the bottom.

Sea Serpent
Tonic

Upon further checking I found out that the best quality snake wine is called the Seven Snake Wine, just as the number of *puttony* designates the quality and richness of the famous Hungarian dessert wine, Tokaj.

I also saw a bottle of Male Silkworm Tonic. The label assured me that the wine was made with virgin male silkworms (as if I didn't know it) from the province of Soutech, bottled in Kwangchow, and used for the treatment of impotence. Every country has its aphrodisiac lore, but when the time comes, I'd rather try the French remedy featuring oysters and caviar.

Other choice selections? A wine made with a gum extract from tortoise shell mixed with antler's horn and a good-tasting herbal wine called Sisian Chen Chiew Tonic from the Hunan province of China. The recipe for the latter comes from the Ming Dynasty and is supposed to strengthen the body and cure approximately a dozen ailments.

I also saw a tonic wine made of glutinous rice recommended "to be used regardless of sex." (The Chinese neatly took care of the entire unisex movement a long time ago.)

Lychee Wine is the Thunderbird of Chinese wines and Tiger Bone Liqueur lists fourteen ingredients and (by tigergum) is made with real tiger bone.

UNGARIAN QUEEN'S WATER

A large variety of fascinating objects has originated in Hungary, although the world has since forgotten the source. To this category belongs the coach (from the Hungarian village "Kocs"); the invention of flour-grinding mills as we know them today (the first to be able to produce snow-white bread) and, most noteworthy, the best mustache wax—even Napoleon III used it.

But the most curious creation of them all is the by-now completely forgotten "Hungarian Queen's Water" (*Aqua Reginae Hungariae*), a miraculous liquid used for the cure of many illnesses, including arthritis of the hands and legs. Joannes Praevotius, physician from Padua, writes in his book published in 1666:

133

As I know the remarkable effectiveness of this medicine, let me tell you how, by chance, I stumbled upon it. Among the books of my good friend F. P. (a Cyprian nobleman), I found in 1606 an extremely old and precious breviary which was given to his ancestors as an expression of especial esteem by St. Elizabeth, Queen of Hungary. On the first page was a prescription for the treatment of arthritis, written in the hand of the queen herself. With the permission of my friend, I wrote it down. Here it is exactly as I found it there:

"I, Elizabeth, Queen of Hungary, when I became very ill and arthritic at the age of seventy-two, used this medicine which was given to me by an old hermit. I had never seen him before nor have I ever seen him again. Soon I became well and was strengthened and rejuvenated—so much that I became so beautiful that the Polish King asked my hand in marriage, since we both had lost our spouses. But my love for my Lord Jesus Christ would not allow me to accept—for it was His angel, I believe, who gave me this medicine."

This is the recipe: Take 3 parts of four-times distilled brandy, 2 parts of the leaf and flower of rosemary. Place in a tightly closed container, keep in a warm place for five hours, then distill and once weekly in your morning drink or food take a drachma, every morning wash your face and the painful limb. It gives back your strength, sharpens the brain, clears the mind and nerves, sharpens the eye, and lengthens life!

Throughout the ages, countless historians and scientists have proven the impossibility of the breviary story, and the incredible claims (among them, that Cramerus and Tomon were rejuvenated at the age of eighty and suddenly were able to perform Polish jigs) made for this concoction. Still, the use of Hungarian Queen's Water was popular for hundreds of years, until the beginning of the nineteenth century, and you can hardly find a household dictionary in any language that does not write with considerable reverence about the powerful effects of this formula or some variation of it.

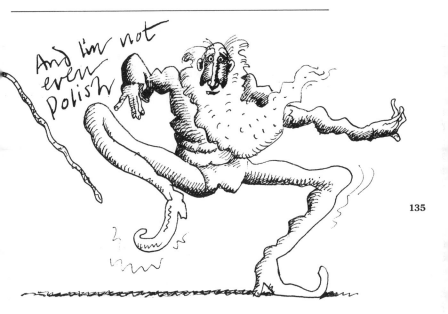

And I'm not even Polish

Here is a version that appeared in the seventeenth century:

Queen of Hungary's Water, The True Way

Take four pounds of Rosemary Flowers, gathered in a fair morning, two or three hours after sunrising and picked from all the green part, put them into a cucurbit, and pour upon them three quarts of Spirit of Wine, well rectified; press down the flowers into the said Spirit, and over the Cucurbit with its Head and Alemback; lute well all the junctures with Paste and Paper then place it in the Sand Bath, and lute a Receiver to it; then leave it so till next Morning; then distill it with so moderate a Fire, that while the Spirit distilleth, the Head may not be so much as warm; or to hasten the Distillation, you may cover the Head with a Linnen Cloth doubled several times and dipped in cold water; dip again, and cool the head several times; continue with the distillation until you have drawn about three quarts of spirit, which will be very pure, and charged with the best and Volatile Substance of the Flowers, then take out all the Fire and let the Bath cool; unlute the Vessels, and put the Spirit into a bottle well stopt; then drain and press out the Liquor that remains in the Cucurbit, and clarifie it, then put it into the Cucurbit again, and distil it until it remain in the bottom of the Consistence near as thick as Honey, or a thick syrup, which put into a Pipkin well glased, and boil it over the Fire to the thickness of an ordinary Extract; put the last Spirit into a Bottle of it self.

BUDDHA JUMPED OVER THE FENCE

The first time I heard about this dish was a couple of years ago in Canton when I was interviewing Mr. Chou, the head chef of the Tung Fang

Hotel. I had asked him what was the most complicated dish
he had ever prepared, and he answered: "Monk Jumping
over the Wall, and it's better than any medicine." He told
me that it originates from the Fukien province of China,

137

where a couple of centuries ago a young monk jumped over the wall of the monastery without permission and for four nights cooked rare delicacies in an earthenware pot. The chief abbot, smelling the incredible aroma, also jumped over the wall and broke his vow of vegetarianism by eating some of the food.

After a lot of useful and useless research I've found not one but three stories about its origin. It is not unlikely that originally it was called Precious Urn with Rare Treasures, or the Nine Delicacies, or Buddha Jumped over the Fence. Its origin may be in Cantonese village festivities where the family got together with friends and steamed pigs' feet and belly, chicken, ham, winter bamboo shoots, shark's fin, and wild mushrooms for seven or eight hours in a porcelain-lined silver and copper urn.

138

According to other records, it originated in the Imperial Palace during the Ching Dynasty (1644–1911) and later was popularized by the immensely wealthy *Taipan* merchants. The food was divided into nine layers and each layer had to be distinctively different and recognizable from the others.

I choose to believe the third version, a rather amusing tale. Some time in the dim past, an especially ingenious family gathered the finest foodstuff the earth, the sky, and the oceans could provide and very slowly steamed it for days in their garden. The aroma wafted over to their next-door neighbor, who happened to be Buddha. He couldn't resist the lingering, teasing fragrance of the sweet juices, and promptly jumped over the neighbor's fence, disregarding temporarily his abstinence from eating living creatures, and zestily joined the feast.

Here is a list of ingredients in case you are planning to prepare it.

1. *Bêche de mer*, also known as sea cucumber, sea slug, marine ginseng, or *hai shen* to the Chinese when used in dried form. This variety is about six inches long and its preparation is long and painstaking. The elongated shape resembles to some degree the genitalia of *both* sexes and, when you see that it contains transparent liquid when cut open, you'll understand why it is believed to be a prime aphrodisiac. (Some cultures believe that foodstuff will be helpful for an organ whose shape it resembles. Stone weed is used to make tea to cure kidney stones for instance, and vanilla became popular as a remedy for women's disorders in Elizabethan times because of the root's resemblance to the vaginal canal.)

Bêche de mer for the Buddha dish is rock hard. It has to be soaked for two days, during which time it will expand about three times. Then it has to be split, scraped, boiled several times, and cleaned, each time discarding the liquid. After this painstaking process, bêche de mer is cooked for three days, at which point it is ready to become an ingredient in the Jumping Buddha dish.

139

2. *Bamboo fungas*, the inner fiber of bamboo. The only type to be used in this dish is grown in the Szechuan province of China. It takes three days to cook.

3. *Fructose Licee*, a dried fruit resembling little shriveled cranberries or terra cotta beads, which is used in many Chinese soups and stews. It's full of vitamin A and supposed to eliminate exhaustion, clear the eyes, cure a cold, act as a laxative, and clean the liver.

4. *Shark's fins*, which take five full days to prepare. The fins are wrapped in cheesecloth to keep their original shape and cooked in water and eventually in stock through a complicated process. Shark's fins contain eighty-three percent protein besides calcium, potassium, and iodine, and they are supposed to protect the liver and kidneys, and clear the lungs.

Unlike in the West, the most expensive Chinese delicacies are colorless, flavorless, and odorless. The silver fungus (see later) and shark's fins are perfect examples of this. These texture foods have no taste of their own; they are like sponges and absorb tastes from other foods or broths. To combine their textures properly is a highly sophisticated art.

5. *Deer sinew* or *deer tendon* (which in dried form looks like odd little sticks carved out of alabaster), which

takes only three days to make. It is pounded, stewed in chicken broth, and finally cooked with sesame oil. When it's finished it looks like a Japanese tickler for especially jaded ladies. It comes from north China and no one thereabout argues that it helps to clarify the blood, fortify bones and tendons, and strengthen the *yang*.

6. *Fresh sea turtle*, weighing about three pounds each.

7. *Dried scallops*, which are extremely high in potassium, iron, and protein, and have more taste than fresh scallops.

8. *Dried abalone*, which clears the blood, takes away "wetness" and poison from the body, and helps one to be more *yang*. It takes twelve hours to cook.

9. *Young shark's air bladder*, cooked for three days. This is a rare texture food, acting as a restorative of bodily vigor.

10. *Snow (or silver) fungi*, a rare tree fungus that may cost as much as $50 an ounce. The list of its medicinal values takes several pages in a Chinese medical encyclopedia, but its two main virtues are that it's supposed to be a curative for heart problems and balance *yin* and *yang*. It also makes you more intelligent.

11. *Dried ginseng*, which comes in a little wooden box. One caddy (a little over a pound) costs $900. The one ounce for our soup cost about $50. It must be from North Korea and, according to hearsay, it has to be uprooted at midnight when the moon is full. I have not seen a Certificate of Correct Harvesting, but I was ready to sample it to avert depression, strengthen my heart, and cure my intellectual problems, as I had once read in a book.

When I first tasted the "Buddha" dish it brought back memories, different ones with each spoonful:

fresh turtle soup I had at a banquet I arranged some years ago at the Savoy in London;

a perfectly reduced consommé the late Albert Stockli once made;

a broth left over from a huge twenty-gallon pot of *bollito misto* (the mixed boiled meats and sausage of North Italy);

the first time I sucked the brains out of a carp's head;

a powdered medicine my mother put into a soup when I was a child and had a high fever.

Epilogue: I am happy to report to you that the day after having three helpings of B.J.O.F. Soup I felt fit as a fiddle.

A DRUNK
BY
ANY OTHER NAME:
THE LANGUAGE
OF
FOOD AND DRINK

CHAPTER
9

Portrait of a Man drinking his buttons off

LE'S WELL THAT ENDS WELL

A person who drinks too much can be called drunk, intoxicated, fuddled, muddled, muzzy, noddy-headed, ginnified, bosky, bemused, cherry-merry, coxy-foxy, chocked or overseen, reely tipsy, merry, half-boosy, half-seas-over (nautical, as in the wind), half-and-half or flatch-kennurd (black slang), top-heavy, cup-sprung, cup-shot, pot-valiant, full of Dutch courage, in his armor, pot-sure, pot-hardy, maudlin, groggy, a jolly-dog; chirping-merry, prime, mellow, spreeish, corked (or corky), rather high-titty, in drink, under the table, or stewed.

"Slued" is of nautical derivation. When a vessel slues it changes the tack and seems to stagger, the sails flap, it gradually keels over, and as the wind catches the waiting canvas, it glides off at another angle. (The analogy is obvious.)

"Gone a peg too low" has an interesting background. The tenth-century Saxon King Edgar, in order to check drunkenness, ordered that pins or nails be fastened into drinking cups or horns at stated distances and that whoever drank beyond these marks at one draught would be liable to severe punishment. The cups or tankards thus marked with pins or pegs, sometimes of gold or silver, were usually called peg-tankards and held two quarts, divided into eight equal portions by seven pegs, one above the other. Each person in turn drank a peg-measure, a restriction that sometimes irked a thirsty or greedy pegger. Edgar's original intention was soon lost, and the pegs intended for the restriction of potations became a provocative challenge to drink, an occasional sport developing into the custom of pin-drinking or pin-nicking, to which we also owe the somewhat dated slang, "He's a merry pin."

It is also said that he who drinks too much and shows the effects has business on both sides of the way, got his little hat on, bung's his eye (possibly drunk on bang juice or beer), been in the sun, got a spur in his head (jockeys use it to each other), got a crumb in his beard, been among the Philistines, lost his legs, been in a storm, got his nightcap on, got his skin full, had his cold tea (tight on brandy), a red eye (on whisky), a pinch of snuff in his wig, taken draps, taken a lunar, had his wig oil'd, been diddled ("diddle" is a synonym for gin), dish'd, and done up.

He clips the King's English, sees double, reels, heels a little, heels and sets, shrews his hobnails, chases geese, cannot sport a right light, can't walk a chalk.

In the 1920s, David Lloyd, a Welshman who kept an inn at Hereford, had a sow with six legs which attracted great numbers of visitors. Apparently Mrs. Lloyd was "much addicted to drunkenness" for which her beloved husband used to bestow on her "very severe drubbing." One day, having taken several extra cups and dreading the usual consequences, she went into the yard, opened the door, and let out the six-legged sow. She lay down in its place, hoping to sleep off her drunkenness. In the meantime, however, curiosity seekers arrived to see the much-talked-about animal with the half dozen pedal extremities. Mr. Lloyd dramatically opened the yard door and, without looking at the animal (since he had seen it enough times), exclaimed: "Did any of you ever see so uncommon a creature before?" "Indeed," said one of the farmers, "I never before observed a sow so very drunk in all of my life!" Thus the saying: "as drunk as David's sow."

Drunk as a lord and drunk as a pope came to us by the grace of His Holiness Benedict XII (pope from 1334–1342), a noted drunkard who also gave rise to the expression *bibamus papaliter* (drinks like a papa).

149

you'd drink too If you had six legs

Fuddled as an ape: Thomas Nashe explains this phrase in his book titled: *Pierce Penilesse, His Supplication to the Divell*:

> We have eight kinds of drunkes. The first is the ape drunke, and he leapes and sings, and hollowes and daunceth for the heavens; the second is Lion drunke, and he flings the pots about the house, calles his Hostesse whore.
>
> The third is Swine drunke, heavy, lumpish, and sleepy, and cries for a little more drinke; the fourth is Sheepe drunke: wise in his own concept, when he cannot bring foorth a right word.
>
> The fifth is Mawdlen drunke, when a fellow will weep for kindness in the midst of his Ale and cries, but the sixth is Martin drunke, when a man drinkes himself sober.
>
> The seventh is goate drunke, when in his drunkenness he has no mind but on lechery.
>
> The eighth is the Foxe drunk when he is a crafty drunk, will never bargain but when he's drunk.

Our inebriated person furthermore may be all mops and brooms, beargered, beery (approaching drunkenness), or be an elbow crooker, wetster, lapper, fiddle-cup, tickle-pitcher, angel-altogether, lug-pot, belch-guts,

150

bang-pitcher, lowerer, rub-pot, wet-subject, dramster or dramist, ale-wisp, blow boll, jolly-nose, swizzle-guts, sipters, nazie cove, swigsby.

Our intemperate tippler could be described as someone who has been talking to Jamie Moore (a Scots expression on the effect of corn juice). Or he has been hit by a barnmouse, is blued, cannon (a tease slang), sparred, disguised (a funny way to be disguised?), flushed (full to the brim), kennurd, all key-hole, hiccius-doccius, hanced (elevated), peekish, swipy, kisky, he has a guest in the attic, his back teeth well afloat, he has a brick in his hat, has the mainbrace well spliced (it means to serve an extra allowance of grog in navy slang), gilded, shot under the wing, muckibus (Irish for sentimental, according to Horace Walpole), scammered, raddled, wet (generic name for booze as in to wet one's whistle), swattled, what-nosed, rammaged, starchy, rosinned, bezzled.

George Jean Nathan, the tart-tongued American theater critic, used to say: "I drink to make other people interesting." He would understand the importance of the words: grape-shot, yaupish, bubbed (got drunk on malt liquor), sossled, palatic (theatrical expression), dagged, bumpsy, stozzled, tap-schackled, whistle-drunk (whistle cup had a whistle attached to it and the last toper capable of using the whistle, received the cup as a prize), taken in a shard, too far north, whipcat, ree-raw, scoop, or bulge.

He may also comparatively be as drunk as a fiddler's bitch (a whore), or drunk as a nurse at a christening, or he may be

151

drinking his buttons off.

Usually it starts with the acceptance of an invitation such as "what will you have?" Perhaps others will ask you "to blink, to damp your mug, to dip your beak, to guttle, to bub, to read the maker's name, to prime yourself, rinse, save a life, shed a tear, sluice your bolt, or soak your chaffer. Or perhaps the invitation will be to scamander, shake a cloth, to take the pin out, wet, tiff, rock, or potate.

After this uncommonly nice invitation has been accepted, you will toast your host or hostess with "Here's into your face!"

The spree itself may be known as breaky-leg, neck-oil, bub, or titley; if you drink it as a nightcap, it may be called by various and sundry individuals as a deoch-an-doras, willy-wacht, big-reposer, or simply a settler. Meantime, before this said event, you may take a nipper, a jorum, bumper, rinse, a short one, or you may have a tift, shant, bullock's eye, sleeve-button, dannie, small cheque, allowance, or lip.

Portrait of
a Man on
a tiffey

153

You are dated as an old fogy by using the word *hooch* for liquor, still, if you're interested it comes from a liquor distilled by the Hoochinoo Indians of Alaska from yeast, flour, and molasses.

Beer has a language of its own, and you may call for reeb, purko, ponge, pongello, never-fear, bivvy, belch, or gatter. A strong ale is variously called hum, knock-down, Pharaoh (based on the questionable theory that the Egyptians invented the art of brewing), October (especially strong brew from the new season's hops).

A small beer is known as down, single-broth, treacle-wag, skin-disease, swish-swash, belly-vengeance, whistle-jacket, bumclink, swanky, slumgullion, and swipes.

If you prefer whisky, you may take your choice and call for poteen, Saint Patrick's well, Fenian, grapple-the-rails, crater, bust-head, ferintosh.

If gin is your drink, then you are for white-lace, blue-tape, tittery, cat water, fuller's earth, nig, cold cream, heart's ease, daffy's elixir, snopsy, rag-water, strip-me-naked.

If rum is the cause of your dipsomania, the words you should be aware of are rumbullion and rumbo while brandy drinkers go for nantz, cold-tea, French article, main-sheet, and yadnarb.

And here is a toast which is offered to the freedom of religion, freedom of the press, freedom of the person under the protection of the Habeas Corpus, and the freedom of calling booze anything you like as long as there is enough of it.

Here's to stout *end*
To bitter *days.*
Ale's *well that ends well.*

155

XCUSE ME, DID YOU SAY KICKSHAW OR QUELQUE CHOSE?

Everybody knows what a coffin is, but it may come as news to you that in medieval cookery, the bakers made a rectangular or oblong-shaped overbaked pastry boat called a *coffin*, which was filled with various stews, fricassees, and ragouts. The coffins were never eaten, only used to hold these stews.

Originally *bread* meant "a little piece" or a fragment. The word for bread was loaf, and only in the Middle Ages did bread come to mean a piece of bread, as today.

Candy comes from the Sanskrit: *Khanda* meant a piece of lump sugar.

Cereal refers to *Ceres*, the protector and goddess of crops.

When a German in the Middle Ages finished his drink, his cup was *gar aus* or totally finished. If he did it too often, he became unruly, and our word *carousing* comes from this derivation.

Julep, like many delicious concoctions, comes from the Arabic, where it meant rosewater.

When you are the lucky participant in an orgy, you are a modern-day follower of the ancient Greeks who turned "secret worship evenings" (*orgia* in Greek) into riotous debauchery.

The *potato* was brought to America in 1719 by a group of Irish Presbyterians. Its origin is a Haitian word, *batata*.

A proper *consommé* needs endless simmering and clarification and the French word *consommer* means "to finish," indicating that a proper consommé is a broth that is truly clarified or finished.

Our Western forefathers liked the Mexican *charquit* (which means dried and sliced in Spanish) and changed the word into jerky (jerked beef).

When you eat in a hash house, presumably chopped up leftovers, remember that the word hash comes from *hacher*, the French word meaning "to chop" (which also gave us the word hatchet).

How about some
corned beef hash
for dinner?

Clove, which does look like a little nail, comes from the Latin *clovis* or nail, and *Khe-tsup*, which in Chinese means a tomato sauce, is the origin of our *ketchup*.

When you've completed your roast course as well as the salad and the cheese service, the table will be cleared for *dessert*. *Desservir* in French means just that, "to clear away."

Since the first specimens came from Tangier, Morocco, we call them *tangerines* instead of mandarin oranges as they're called in most European countries.

The word *sukiyaki* comes from the Japanese word *suki* which means spade. The Japanese farmers used to grill their fish and later meat on a hoe or spade while working the fields. (They only started eating beef after 1936.)

158

Man obsessed
by authenticity
cooking
sukiyaki
at home

Many of the Gaelic names in the Scottish cuisine are distortions of the French, like "tartar purry," which comes from *tarte en purée*, and a "kickshaw" originally was *quelque chose*, a garnish consisting of asparagus, truffles, mushrooms, lemon slices, and pistachios.

The distinction *cordon bleu* is used freely today to describe everything from Martell's Cognac to prime ribs of beef to a cooking school and several dozen supposedly eminent items in between. Actually the title *cordon bleu* was first bestowed by Madame de Maintenon, mistress of Louis XIV, at a school in St. Cyr that was established to educate the orphan daughters of noble officers. The students were instructed in the culinary arts, and those who excelled received Cordon Bleu, i.e., the blue ribbon.

159

According to the popular etymologist Willard R. Espy, in his delightful book, *O Thou Improper, Thou Uncommon Noun* (Clarkson N. Potter, 1978), *pumpernickel* might have received its name during an invasion of Eastern Europe when Napoleon was offered the stuff by local peasants. He tasted it, screwed up his face, and passed the bread to his horse, Nicole, saying, *"Bon pour Nicole"* —good enough, that is, for a horse. Hence by sound association, pum-per-nickel. Mr. Espy says that others, however, trace pumpernickel to the German *pumper*, colloquially meaning "to fart," since the bread has this effect on some people, and *nickel*, colloquially "the devil."

The heart, liver, and lungs of a deer had a specific name in the Middle Ages; they were called *numbles*. After the hunt, the ladies and gentlemen ate spit-roasted baron or tenderloin of venison, while the servants had the innards. To make it more palatable they cleverly baked it into a pie first called *Numble Pie* or *Umble Pie*, and later changed into *Humble Pie*. The servants ate what was unacceptable to their masters and somewhere along the mysterious roadways of etymology, when you had to admit a humiliating mistake, you were forced to eat *Humble Pie*.

When I came to America and first heard this expression, I thought it referred to inexpensive pie, made with cheap filling. Little did I know . . .

160

L ET'S GO TO KIDNEY PUNCH AT THE RUB-A-DUB-DUB

Originally a Cockney was a simple country person, a "rube," as he's called in some parts of the United States.

A misshapen egg was also called a cockney in England.

Everybody knows now that a Cockney is a Londoner born within the sound of Bow Bells (St. Mary-le-Bow Church)

who speaks a rhyming slang developed to outwit the
authorities and anyone else felt to be an eavesdropper.

Here is a Cockney food and drink sampler:

Aristotle	bottle
Army and Navy	gravy
Babbling Brook	crook
Bazaar	bar
Battle-cruiser	boozer
Conan Doyle	boil
Doctor Crippen	bread and dripping
Gay and Grisky	whisky
Fine and Dandy	brandy
Jim Skinner	dinner
Kate and Sydney	steak and kidney
Kidney Punch	lunch
Lilly and Skinner	dinner
Pig's Ear	beer (I like me glass of pig's)
Rub-a-dub-dub	pub
Stand at Ease	cheese
Tom Thumb	rum
Uncle Fred	bread
You and Me	tea

161

based on RHYMING COCKNEY SLANG, edited by Jack Jones, Abson Wick, Bristol,
England: Abson Books, 1971.

EATING Is BELIEVING:
TRUE FANTASTIC
STORIES
ABOUT FOOD
CHAPTER
10

cold chicken

NE B-L-T TO GO, HOLD THE MAYO

Michelangelo worked in Carrara marble, Siegel likes plaster, and Rudy Giacomo does his masterpieces in food. As Steve Chawkins reported in the *Atlantic Monthly* in February 1977, Giacomo is planning his chef d'oeuvre by making a thirty-nine-mile-long manicotti and circling Manhattan with its five-feet diameter tubular shape. It will weigh roughly 3½ million pounds and will require all the ricotta cheese produced in the middle-Atlantic states for three weeks before the stuffing will take place.

How will it be baked? The solution is the world's longest, custom-made continuous heating coil. Forty-two industrial vacuum pumps will transfer 2,000 gallons of cheese per minute from tankers in the East River, and two dozen New York City fire trucks will be stationed at points beside the noodle to wash away an anticipated seven tons of cheese spillage.

You certainly cannot have manicotti without tomato sauce, and fifty-two crop-dusting planes will take care of this problem by dropping 30,000 gallons of tomato sauce along the way. Also, 4,200 security guards armed with flyswatters and mousetraps plus loaded Smith & Wesson .38s will keep bugs, rodents, and other vandals behind the purple velvet rope around the unending manicotti.

Then comes the glorious moment: security guards will be released and Manhattanites will step forward and devour the manicotti.

No one mentions the amount of medicine which will be necessary the following day; Alka-Seltzer, Bromo Seltzer, and competing brands will be selling at a premium.

If you think that this is just a thirty-nine-mile-long pipe dream, you have a thing or two coming to you. Because Giacomo is ready to build a twenty-four-story middle-income apartment building in Chicago out of Ritz crackers and peanut butter; in 1961 he lined a two-mile stretch of the coastline of southwest Africa with elaborate interweaving trails of salami and eggs. The art encyclopedias of day-after-tomorrow will record his feat as *Two Over Easy* and will mention the fact that aesthetically inclined wild beasts consumed it in a very short time after it was completed.

I personally would like to be shipwrecked with the seventeen-foot-high tuna sandwich he exhibited in his front yard in Staten Island that he titled *Spare the Mayo*.

HINK BIG

Although the *Guinness Book of World Records* does not mention it, I believe that the largest punch bowl ever assembled was by an Admiral Edward Russell, commander of the Mediterranean fleet, who in 1694 transformed a marble fountain in Alicante, Spain, into an enormous punch bowl for a party. To give you an idea of the size, they needed 2,500 lemons and 20 gallons of lime juice to give the proper flavor to the hundreds of gallons of alcohol. A young boy was selected to sit in a tiny boat and ladle out the punch to the 6,000 people invited to this ingenious entertainment.

NTER LAUGHING

I have no reason not to believe this bit of reportage in a book called *London at Table*, published in 1851. Weight Watchers won't like it, but I shall quote a paragraph:

167

I know a club of fat men that did not come together (as you may well suppose) to entertain one another with sprightliness and wit, but to keep one another in countenance. The room where the club met was something of the largest, and had two entrances, one by a door of moderate size, and the other by a pair of folding-doors. If a candidate for this corporate club could make his entrance through the first, he was looked upon as unqualified: but if he stuck in the passage, and could not force his way through it, the folding doors were immediately thrown open for his reception, and he was saluted cheerfully as a brother.

168

I AM THE FRIENDLY GREEN PICKLE

Who installed an 800-pound, fourteen-and-a-half-foot, 150-year-old alligator in a glass tank atop his factory building, hoping that his employees would enjoy the sight as much as he did? Answer: H. J. Heinz, the founder of the pickle empire in 1898, in Pittsburgh, of course. He belongs in a book of firsts, for being the advertising genius who in 1900 installed New York's first electric sign six stories above the corner of Fifth Avenue and Twenty-third Street. It was a giant green pickle, forty feet long—with the name Heinz in the center—using 1,200 Mazda bulbs at a time when very few homes had even a single light bulb.

ould you believe the original Heinz Alligator Pickle?

169

ND SERVED WITH HUNDRED THOUSAND ISLAND DRESSING?

The *New York Times* reported that on a 90-degree summer day in Albany, New York, the state and a local supermarket built what may be the world's largest salad in the middle of the Empire State Plaza.

A total of 6,600 heads of crisp iceberg lettuce, 38,000 cherry tomatoes, 750 pounds of red onions, and 200 pounds of red cabbage—all grown in New York State—were trucked in huge plastic trash bags to the center of the marbled office complex. About half of it was tossed in a twenty-four-foot swimming-pool-turned-salad-bowl atop a ton and a half of ice.

There it was left to wilt, along with hundreds of bemused state employees and curious passers-by who lined up for free samples. Their salads—12,000 were prepared—came in individually wrapped bowls, since serving the supersalad itself might have violated health regulations, despite a ycllow- and white-striped canopy constructed to keep low-flying birds away.

170

The record-breaking leftovers were donated to a nearby farm as food for cattle.

F ORTY-FOUR THOUSAND PIZZAS DIED IN VAIN

The Associated Press reported that in Alpena, Michigan, 44,000 frozen mushroom pizzas were buried by Mario Fabbrini because the federal government believed the mushrooms used were tainted with botulism toxin. Mr. Fabbrini dutifully called the pizzas back from stores when two test mice died after eating samples of the pizza. It was discovered later that the mice did not die of botulism.

"I think it was indigestion. Maybe they didn't like my pizza," said Mr. Fabbrini.

But by then the pizzas had all been collected and buried on a nearby farm. At the burial were Mr. Fabbrini's twenty-two employees and several newsmen, and the governor of Michigan spoke. Mr. Fabbrini placed a wreath of red gladioli and white carnations on the grave of the pizzas, which he valued at $39,000.

After the burial, those present were offered a repast of—what else?—pizza. When a reporter demurred, Mr. Fabbrini said "the Governor ate a piece, and he's still alive."

171

Mr. Fabbrini is suing the distributor of the mushrooms for a million dollars.

EAVY ON THE KETCHUP

According to the Associated Press one Libby Thomas, a twenty-three-year-old Texan, won a hamburger eating contest in that state, vanquishing seven men as she put away thirteen burgers in an hour and a half. Her secret? She warmed up before the contest by eating thirteen tunafish sandwiches and two cakes. Ms. Thomas weighs 120 pounds.

O THAT'S WHERE IT GOES

One warm spring day recently Ringling Brothers and Barnum & Bailey Circus had a giant manure giveaway at Madison Square Garden in New York. As one might imagine, mineral-rich manure is generated in gargantuan proportions by the circus's herd of eighteen elephants, dozens of horses, and other hay-eating animals.

The possibilities in the vegetable garden are fantastic. Zebra manure could produce striped tomatoes perfect for the chef who has trouble slicing in straight lines; a plant treated with camel manure could go for days without water; and the use of elephant manure could result in cucumbers the size of watermelons!

OMMY, MOMMY, WHERE IS MY MUFFLER?

The U.S. Department of Agriculture (talk about culinary nonsense) reportedly tried to develop featherless chickens that would not have to be plucked. Unfortunately, it turned out that these poor birds caught colds very easily and so, to date, the future of the project is highly questionable.

B UT DID IT RECEIVE THE AMERICAN DENTAL ASSOCIATION'S APPROVAL?

In May 1978 three Georgia farmers decided to try mixing cement dust with cattle feed. Cement is rich in calcium, and their steers gained weight at double the rate of conventionally fed stock. The U.S. Department of Agriculture has confirmed the experiments, according to the *Daily Mail*, but isn't saluting a breakthrough until it discovers what happens when people eat concrete steaks.

173

C AT-ASTROPHE

United Press International reported in June 1976 that Ray McPherson of Miami was very disturbed when he discovered that an employee in the temporary office services company he ran had taken to eating a few spoonfuls of cat food on his break. What especially bothered him was the brand.

"I've never smelled anything so bad," McPherson said. "This guy would stink up the whole place in minutes. I wouldn't even feed it to a cat."

McPherson fired the unnamed employee, but ran afoul of

the government in doing so. The man went to the Equal Employment Opportunity Commission and said he ate the cat food because of his religious convictions and that, therefore, he was being discriminated against.

"And they're actually pursuing it," McPherson said.

UT HOW MANY DOLLY PARTONS ARE THERE?

In 1969 Lord Snowdon produced a BBC-TV documentary showing a live chicken that supposedly had been incubated in the bosom of a sixty-year-old housewife. One viewer objected, stating that an egg could only be hatched in a 104-degree environment and that from his "experience of ladies' bosoms, this is rarely attainable." However, according to the Poultry and Egg Institute of America, "an egg can hatch at 98.6 degrees, although 100 degrees is optimum." I wonder if this information will start a new craze . . .?

HIPS WITH EVERYTHING

The bill of fare in fashionable London restaurants today is so varied that it is easy to forget that mainstay of the English diet, chips.

Noted English playwright Arnold Wesker titled his 1962 play *Chips with Everything*, and the London *Daily Telegraph*, in its January 2, 1980, issue, printed an extract from the menu displayed in a café near the Basingstoke bus station:

Egg and Chips
Two Eggs and Chips
Egg, Bacon and Chips
Two Eggs, Bacon and Chips
Sausage and Chips
Two Sausages and Chips
Bacon, Sausage and Chips
Egg, Sausage and Chips
Egg, Two Sausages and Chips
Two Eggs, Sausage and Chips
Two Eggs, Two Sausages and Chips
Egg, Bacon, Sausage and Chips
Two Eggs, Bacon, Sausage and Chips
Egg, Bacon, Two Sausages and Chips
Two Eggs, Bacon, Two Sausages and Chips
Egg, Bacon, Sausage, Beefburger and Chips

LASPHEMY!

A diner at an Ontario hotel was apparently so enraged by the toughness of his Yorkshire pudding that he impaled it on his fork, marched into the kitchen, and said: "I want whoever cooked this to eat it."

The chef, taken aback, eventually replied, "You're not supposed to eat a Yorkshire pudding. It's purely for decoration."

 # UT ONE DAY HE'LL GO TOO FAR . . .

In 1956 a Parisian night watchman named Noel Carriou got so angry because his wife made the roast too rare that, after a heated argument following the dinner, he literally kicked her out of bed with such vehemence that she broke her neck and died. Carriou served seven years at hard labor, then got out of prison and married again.

One day, Clemence, his second wife, erred in the opposite direction and overcooked his roast. "You cook like a Nazi," he screamed, and promptly picked up a kitchen knife and stabbed her to death.

The French jury, showing sympathy for Carriou's exacting

food tastes (crime of gastronomic passion) sentenced him to only eight years behind bars.

EWS ITEMS OF COSMIC INTEREST

Did you know that it is against the law (a) to sell cornflakes on Sunday in Columbus, Ohio, (b) to slurp soup in a public restaurant in New Jersey, (c) to ride any bus or attend any theater in Gary, Indiana, within four hours after eating garlic?

LL THE WORLD'S FIGHTING BEERS

A three-man crew actually sailed from Australia to Singapore in a beer-can hull ship called the *Can-Tiki*. The skipper, Clem Jones, said that sailing a beer-can vessel had advantages because buoyancy could be increased at any time simply by drinking the beer. Jones said he had never handled a boat before but found it no problem. "Steering at night is no different from steering in the daytime," he said, "except you can't see."

The crew has plans to launch a beer-can aircraft carrier sometime in the future and hasn't given up hope on their cherished dream: a beer-can submarine. They built one once and it did submerge, but failed to surface again. They are trying to work the bugs out.

AEL GREENE, WHERE WERE YOU WHEN WE NEEDED YOU?

Phyllis Magida and Bob Schwabach of the *Chicago Tribune* collect some of the most titillating, though unchewable, tidbits for her column, and with her permission, I pass on to you this tip: If you want to eat in an unusual atmosphere, you should go to a place called Adam and Eve in Naked City, Indiana, where everybody—the chef, the waiters, and even the patrons—appear in the buff. She gave three stars for ambiance but couldn't recall the food, so she hasn't rated that for the time being.

INDEX

184

ABOUT THE AUTHOR

GEORGE LANG is a man of many talents. Hungarian born, he began his professional life as a violinist and at the age of twenty entered the gastronomic field, where he has been ever since. Today, he is described as "the man who invents restaurants" (*Fortune*), hailed as "a world expert on culinary affairs" (*London Sunday Telegraph*) and "a restaurateur of grand repute" (*The New Yorker*).

After studying in Europe, Lang came to the United States. Beginning as a cook for $46 a week, he soon became a noted chef-saucier and chef-decorator for a number of fine restaurants here and abroad. One of his many career highlights occurred in 1957, when Lang arranged a legendary state dinner for Queen Elizabeth II at the Waldorf-Astoria.

During the 1960s Lang ran New York's famous Four Seasons restaurant, in addition to developing many successful Restaurant Associates establishments. He lectured at the Hotel School in Cuba and was the first restaurateur to visit mainland China. In 1970 he founded the George Lang Corporation, an international consulting firm, which has been described as "the only think tank in the food and beverage industry." Over the last ten years he has been involved in developing projects all over the world, from a resort complex in

Thessalonica, Greece, to the Citicorp Market in New York City.

As a writer, his *The Cuisine of Hungary* is regarded as the definitive volume on the subject, and his "Table for One" column is a monthly feature in *Travel & Leisure* magazine. Lang has also contributed articles to the *New York Times Magazine, Esquire, Bon Appetit, Hospitality,* and other major publications.

Lang runs two top restaurants in Manhattan: Café des Artistes, just off Central Park West, and Hungaria, in the new Citicorp Center.

Among his other talents, Lang is an expert calligrapher (his work was exhibited at the Museum of American Folk Art in 1975), and he is currently working on a roman à clef about the food industry.

Lang shares his offices in Manhattan with a staff of nine and two cats, Truffles and Escoffier.

MILTON GLASER is a renowned artist, illustrator, and designer. A cofounder of *New York* magazine and Push Pin Studios, he has been awarded the Society of Illustrators Gold Medal, the Art Directors Club Gold Medal, and the Saint-Gauden's Medal from the Cooper Union. He has had numerous museum exhibitions in ten countries, including shows at the Pompidou Palace in Paris and the Museum of Modern Art in New York. Recently he designed sections of the Sesame Street Children's Park near Philadelphia.

WILLIAM SAFIRE is a Pulitzer Prize—winning columnist for the *New York Times,* a best-selling novelist, and a dedicated lexicographer.

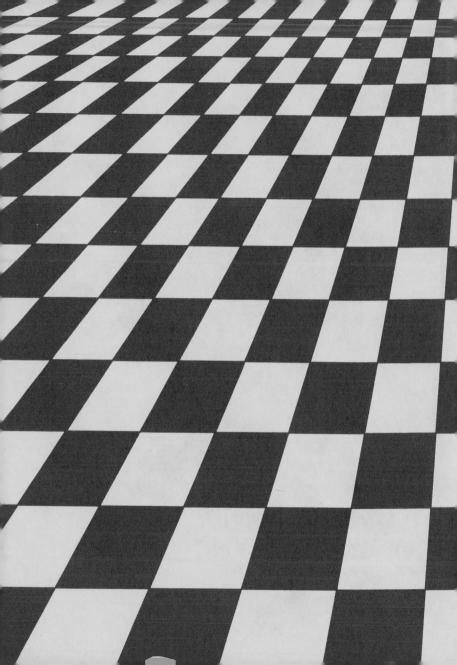